A GREAT

AWAKENING

IS COMING!

A GREAT
AWAKENING
IS COMING!

#1 *NEW YORK TIMES* BESTSELLING AUTHOR
MIKE EVANS

TIMEWORTHY BOOKS

P.O. BOX 30000, PHOENIX, AZ 85046

I dedicate this book to a man of God
who impacted my life
the late David Wilkerson . . .
. . . it was he not me that was the
inspiration for this book.

Carolyn and I began our ministry running
Teen Challenge which he founded several months
after we married in Arkansas in 1970. The first book
I ever read was *The Cross and the Switchblade*.

David Wilkerson founded World Challenge, Inc. in 1971
to reach the lost and strengthen believers around the
globe. Both leading up to the start of World Challenge
and in the years after, he was faithfully obedient to
follow God and minister to others in love and deed.

Prior to founding World Challenge, David Wilkerson
was called to New York in 1958 to minister to gang
members and drug addicts, as told in the best-selling
book, *The Cross and the Switchblade*. Not long after,
Teen Challenge was birthed; this addiction recovery
ministry expanded across the country within a
few years and eventually around the world.

CONTENTS

"THE PEOPLE
THAT DO KNOW
THEIR GOD
SHALL BE STRONG,
AND DO
EXPLOITS."

-DANIEL 11:32, KJV

INTRODUCTION
....

Will you not revive us again,

that your people may rejoice in you?

—PSALM 85:6, ESV

A GREAT AWAKENING is within us, waiting to be stirred up as it was in the first followers of Jesus on the Day of Pentecost! Awakening is not merely a concert featuring large crowds, enthusiasm, repentance, or powerful worship. If we define "revival" as simply a state of being revived, quickened, or filled with God's presence, and not split hairs over the word, we can say that Christ lived on earth in perpetual revival. He was filled with the presence of the Father. That's why when He saw a widow's grief (Luke 7) at the loss of her only son, Jesus reached out and touched the dead boy, who instantly sprang to life. That's true awakening!

Spiritual awakening happens to believers when they refuse to live complacent and begin to hunger and thirst for God. They won't settle for anything but Him.

The recent coronavirus has not taken God by surprise. He is at work through this pandemic to revive and restore His people. His power and glory will shake the world and take us beyond Pentecost to a true Great Awakening.

1

A WORD FROM THE LORD

Go, my people, enter your rooms and shut the doors behind you;
hide yourselves for a little while until his wrath has passed by.
See, the LORD is coming out of his dwelling to punish the people of
the earth for their sins. The earth will disclose the blood shed on
it; the earth will conceal its slain no longer.

—ISAIAH 26:20-21

GOD HAS GIVEN ME a word that has shaken me to my knees.

As I was working on this revelation that God put in my heart, I picked up an old Bible, and a handwritten note fell out. It was from a meeting I had with Dr. David Wilkerson at the Embassy Suites near the Dallas-Fort Worth Airport on a Tuesday in 1986 when we were having breakfast. The letter he wrote was addressed to Rev. Richard Dortch, who ran PTL under Jim Bakker.

It said, "Within 12 months from the date of this letter, the judgment of God will fall on PTL. You are fornicating with brick and stone. Flee now and repent. Bats will fly through the empty building."

It was exactly 12 months to the day that the *Charlotte Observer* broke the PTL scandal story.

In that meeting in 1986, Dr. Wilkerson said something else to me: "I see a plague coming on the world, and the bars and churches and government will shut down. The plague will hit New York City and shake it like it has never been shaken. The plague is going to force prayerless believers into radical prayer and into their Bibles, and repentance will be the cry from the man of God in the pulpit. And out of it will come a third Great Awakening that will sweep America and the world."

I have a word from God for you and it will change your life if you receive it. I hear preachers frequently mentioning that they have "a word from God." I hardly ever say this, because I believe it is a very sobering thing to say. Others say, "I have a prophetic word." I usually don't say that either, but this is indeed a prophetic word from the Lord. It's the hardest message I've ever shared.

What is this message? The coronavirus will usher in a Great Awakening.

The prophet Jeremiah said, "'I will not mention his word or speak anymore in his name,' his word is in my heart like a fire, a fire shut up in my bones" (Jeremiah 20:9). Jesus added, "When you see all these things, you know that it is near, right at the door" (Matthew 24:33).

You're seeing the COVID-19 coronavirus spreading around the world, impacting people in your community. Like many, you may be asking yourself, "Is there any prophetic significance to any of this?"

Romans 8:22 says, "For we know that the whole creation has been groaning as in the pains of childbirth right up to the present time." It describes it as an intimate groaning together, earnestly wanting and wishing to be delivered. The whole creation seems to wait with earnest expectation for a period when the children of God shall be manifested in the glory prepared for them.

That is a tremendous revelation. That word translated "groaning" is an expression of universal grief. It's a worldwide lament in which a dying world unites. Is that happening now? You better believe it's going on now. It's also to suffer the pains of childbirth. The travailing over the distress. And then another word we use: "together." It refers to the complex whole of creation. Then the word "now." The "now" specifically refers to His glory, something magnificent God is going to do.

In 2 Chronicles 7, Solomon dedicated the temple. The Bible says fire from heaven consumed the burnt offering and the sacrifice and the glory of the Lord filled the temple so greatly that the priest could not enter it. Isn't that amazing? Think of that as your church. Imagine you are dedicating your church and the glory of the Lord is filling the place so greatly you can't even stand His presence.

Then the Lord appeared to Solomon at night and said, "I have heard your prayers and have chosen this place for myself as a temple for sacrifices" (2 Chronicles 7:12). Everyone was excited at what God was doing that day. They experienced His glory in a powerful way. Yet on the same day, God also told Solomon, "When I shut up the heavens so that there is no rain, or command locusts to devour the land or send a plaque among my people. . . (2 Chronicles 7:13)." Suddenly, the attitude has changed. Verse 14 adds, ". . .if my people, who are called by my name, will humble themselves and pray and seek my face and turn from their wicked ways, I will hear from heaven, and I will forgive their sin and will heal their land" (2 Chronicles 7:14).

Now this is a tough one. I feel like Jeremiah when he spoke the word of the Lord and people rejected it. People scoffed at him. They could not receive what he was saying.

I want you to see something else from Matthew 24. Jesus departs from the temple and the disciples, and the disciples came to Him talking about the greatness of the temple. It was very similar to what happened with Solomon. It's like two church dedications. They were looking at this glorious temple. They are saying, "Look at this, Jesus. Isn't fantastic? Isn't our worship great? Isn't our preaching great?"

What did Jesus say? Similar to God's words to Solomon, Jesus answered, "Truly I tell you, not one stone here will be left on another; every one will be thrown down" (Matthew 24:2). Here are two dedications. Both were disrupted by a manifested presence of God. Shocking!

Jesus continued as they sat on the Mount of Olives. I have been to the Mount of Olives. It's an amazing place. They came to Him privately, asking, ". . .when will this happen, and what will be the sign of your coming and of the end of the age?" (Matthew 24:3).

In Luke 21:28, the answer Jesus gave reads, "When these things begin to take place, stand up and lift up your heads, because your redemption is drawing near." I don't see a lot of people in the middle of the coronavirus standing up, lifting up their heads, rejoicing that their redemption is drawing near. Yet God's Word does not create panic. People who have been with Jesus are prepared for storms.

THE PROPHETIC SIGNIFICANCE OF THE CORONAVIRUS

Does the Coronavirus have a prophetic significance? The answer is yes. Isaiah prophesied that God will shake the whole earth. God is going to lay waste the earth and devastate it. Hebrews 12:26-27 says:

> "Once more I will shake not only the earth but also the heavens." The words "once more" indicate the removing of what can be shaken—that is, created things—so that what cannot be shaken may remain.

Everything that can be shaken is being shaken. This includes the economy that people have put their faith in. This includes political systems, as many people have trusted in the government over God. This includes education, as schools are shut down and millions of children are now at home. Even our churches have been shut down.

We have never had a time like this in our nation. Everything we have put our security in is being shaken. All our idols are coming down.

Do we have idols in our lives? Yes. An idol is anything that gets between us and God. Anything! It could be money or family or shopping or sports or fame or education or status. Whatever we treasure and consumes us is an idol. It could even be your church. It could even be your pastor.

GOD AT WORK IN INDIA

Let me tell you something that happened that opened my spirit to this revelation in a great way. Many years ago, I flew with my daughter to Madras, India. I flew there to hold my first crusade and Shira said to me, "Daddy, are you going to preach to many people?"

I said, "Sure, I am going to preach to a million."

She said, "A million?"

I said, "Yes, we set up lights and a sound system on a beach for a million people to gather."

She said, "Daddy, have you ever been to India."

I said, "Never." And she looked at me like with a puzzling gaze.

That night I went to sleep and had a dream. It was a God dream. I saw the throne room of God. I saw the Lord in the dream and the Lord looked at me. Then he looked down and in front of me were idols, big ones and fat ones and skinny ones and thin ones. He said to me, "Whose idols are these?" I knew. They were the idols of the Indian people. I started to open my mouth, but then I looked and saw the idols more closely. Every one of them had my name on them!

I woke up crying. I could not breathe. It was 1:30 in the morning. I felt like a dead man. I spent the rest of the night in prayer, feeling unclean and dirty. I had seen the Lord and He had shown me the idols in my life.

The next day I told my team, "I cannot preach. God has shown me things. I can't preach."

They said, "You have to, they have come to hear you." I went out to the stadium that night. There were not a million people there. The crowd included maybe 30,000 Hindus. I put my sermon down because I knew God did not want me to share it. He said, "Say, 'See Jesus.'"

I obeyed. I said, "See Jesus!" I shared a few more words and again felt the Lord encourage me to say, "See Jesus." I started saying a few more words and then did it for a third time, "See Jesus." After I had said these words for the third time, my associate came up, grabbed the microphone, and said, "Stop preaching."

I handed the microphone to a Hindu doctor who was crying. He said, "I am an eye doctor. I have little girls from my blind school who were born blind. Now three of them are seeing! When you said, 'See Jesus,' no one touched them, but their eyes were opened. They started screaming and crying, saying, 'We can see, we can see!'"

It was unbelievable. I returned home that night and rejoiced. I said, "God, you are so astonishing. I repent of my wicked ways and Your glory heals three little girls miraculously." That story hit all the Indian wire services. The next morning, when I woke for breakfast, I opened my door. I could not get out. The Speaker of the House for the Indian Parliament, a Hindu, with his Muslim assistant who had multiple sclerosis, were standing in front of my door asking for prayer.

The line stretched down the stairs and out into the street! I prayed for hours for people.

That evening when I walked outside there were thousands of people wanting me to stretch out my hand and bless them. Then when I arrived at our outreach even, that huge beach area that was empty the night before included over a million people there that night hungry for Jesus.

DO NOT BE DECEIVED

Let's return to Matthew 24. In verse 4, Jesus says, "Watch out that no one deceives you. For many will come in my name." Now what does He mean by "my name"? In the Greek it means reputation, authority, and fame. Many will come in My reputation, in My authority, and My fame and will deceive many. Many will come? This will take place before His return.

Verse 5 adds, "For many will come in my name, claiming I. . ." Do you know what the Greek word for "I" is? E-G-O. He is saying many will come in My reputation, authority, and fame as a strong personality, using a false anointing to deceive many.

Let's look at the word "deceived." It reminds me of an interesting account in Acts 19:13-16:

> Some Jews who went around driving out evil spirits tried
> to invoke the name of the Lord Jesus over those who
> were demon-possessed. They would say, "In the name of

the Jesus whom Paul preaches, I command you to come out." Seven sons of Sceva, a Jewish chief priest, were doing this. One day the evil spirit answered them, "Jesus I know, and Paul I know about, but who are you?" Then the man who had the evil spirit jumped on them and overpowered them all. He gave them such a beating that they ran out of the house naked and bleeding.

That is an early example of the deception Jesus mentions in Matthew 24. We cannot put our faith in man. We must put our faith in God. Faith in man that is exalted is idolatry, even if it is in your pastor. What? Yes! Even if it is in your pastor. You can't even make your church something that becomes so obsessive that it becomes all consuming. If it does, it is an idol.

GOD IS SHAKING THE CHURCH

I can tell you God is shaking the church. He is shaking it to be the body of Christ. We are not spectators or fans glorifying the pulpit. It breaks my heart to say this, but God shut down the church. The government did not do it. God did. He shut our churches down so God's people would get on their faces and pray and repent. He shut them down so God's people would get in the Word.

Most believers are not in the Word. You rarely even see a person carrying a Bible to church today. You know what they use as an excuse? Oh, I use my smart phone. Yes, you use your phone for a lot of things. Many use it to watch pornography, but are you are reading the Word of God? You are not burning with the fire of God and God is saying I am going to drive you to a place where you will have to seek my face. You have no choice. All your idols, I am pulling down.

I have had the privilege of ministering to pastors because I have preached in over 4,000 churches. Over the years, I have had pastors tell me things in confidence. One megachurch pastor admitted he was having an affair and was addicted to porn. Another pastor of a large congregation told me, "I have not prayed in twenty years." He said, "I only pray in public and I only read my Bible for the sermons. I have no devotional life and no prayer life."

Another pastor confessed, "I have been mad at one of my church members for years. I hate him." Another megachurch pastor told me he was an alcoholic. A pastor even once told me he had kicked a board member out of his church, and was so arrogant that he smiled and said he had a doggie door for the man if he ever stepped foot in his church again. As a pastor, how can you talk like that?

One time I shared a word from God with the pastor from one of America's largest churches. It was not an easy message, but it was truly from God. Later, I was in a store and my phone rang. He called me screaming and cursing and threatening to beat me up. I'll never forget it. He said, "Nobody talks to me like that."

This is not the way of the Lord. Jesus said in Matthew 7:21-23, "Not everyone who says to me, 'Lord, Lord,' will enter the kingdom of heaven, but only the one who does the will of my Father who is in heaven. Many will say to me on that day, 'Lord, Lord, did we not prophesy in your name and in your name drive out demons and in your name perform many miracles?' Then I will tell them plainly, 'I never knew you. Away from me, you evildoers!'"

In the original Greek language, the word "evildoer" referred to a worker of iniquity or a worker of lawlessness. They are a law unto themselves. It is like an invisible virus. Remember what Satan said to Eve? Let me paraphrase. "Hey Eve, God is easy. He loves you. He won't punish you for disobeying." You know what that is? That is exactly the theme of the seeker-friendly church in America. It's a gospel of accommodation, accommodating Sodom and Gomorrah to fill the pews. It's a gospel that doesn't preach against sin and doesn't speak about immorality. The immoral feel comfortable in the church.

That is why the divorce rate is as high outside the church as inside it. Pastor, when was the last time God called you to repent? You tell your stories of success, but a lot of those are self-inspired narratives. By the way, that is an acronym for S.I.N. (self-inspired narratives). You only tell the part that makes you look good. You don't want to tell them the rest of the stuff.

Satan is seducing the masses with entertainment. God's house is not a house of prayer. Why are we lying about this? If Jesus came into the average church in America, He would turn over the tables like he did in the temple because it's not a place of prayer. There is not red hot prayer taking place there. At best, there is a quick prayer at the end if you want someone to pray for you, but there's no crying out to God for revival in brokenness and repentance.

Pastor, God does not need your sermons. Many times, His word to you in the pulpit is to shut up. Your slick program hasn't worked. You have programmed everything to accommodate everyone. If the Holy Ghost showed up in power, He could not get in. There is no room in your program!

A LESSON FROM LONDON

One time, I was going to speak at a very famous revival church, Kensington Temple in London, and I had a sore throat. I did something dumb. I got on motorcycle in shorts without a helmet. I was only going a half a mile to get some throat medicine, but as I crossed the red light, a young kid and a teenager in a pickup ran the light and came right at my motorcycle. I had to lay the motorcycle down and slid across the asphalt as the tar burned my arm and my leg. I thought, "God, the devil is attacking me. He is attacking me because you put a great message on my heart and the devil is trying to keep me from sharing it."

When I got to London, I stood outside, and there was a cab stopped. British cabs are higher up and the mirror on the cab hit me on the shoulder and knocked me down. My shoulder was black and blue. So, I finally arrived at the church with a great message God had given me, but I was covered with bruises on my right arm, my left arm, and both legs. I knew it was all the devil, because he

did not want me to share my message. I started preaching from
Luke 4:16-20:

> He went to Nazareth, where he had been brought up,
> and on the Sabbath day he went into the synagogue, as
> was his custom. He stood up to read, and the scroll of the
> prophet Isaiah was handed to him. Unrolling it, he found
> the place where it is written:
>
> "The Spirit of the Lord is on me,
> > because he has anointed me
> > to proclaim good news to the poor.
> He has sent me to proclaim freedom for the prisoners
> > and recovery of sight for the blind,
> to set the oppressed free,
> > to proclaim the year of the Lord's favor."
>
> Then he rolled up the scroll, gave it back to the attendant
> and sat down. The eyes of everyone in the synagogue
> were fastened on him.

That was my text for Kensington Temple. Then I was going to
preach this incredible message God had given me, but I tried to open
my mouth, God told me to stop speaking and sit down. The pastor
looked at me wondering what was wrong. He never spoke and I never
spoke. The next few moments were some of the most miserable minutes of my life. Everyone in the congregation of several thousand

people were looking around and wondering what was wrong. Then in the back, it was as if someone had blown the doors out, and the Holy Spirit started coming down the rows of the cathedral.

People started crying and weeping. Three pastors repented of immorality. The power came and kept moving toward the front of the room. I have never felt such power. The pastor near me fell flat on his back. A revival broke out that shook London and much of Europe because I shut my mouth and obeyed God.

How is it possible today, brothers and sisters, that believers can go to R-rated movies and they don't feel convicted, but instead comfortable? How is it possible that the lost don't have to go to bars anymore to pick up girls? They can go to church. The Spirit of God is saying that your golden calves are coming down. It's time to repent. The Spirit is saying to build your house upon the rock. Repent in prayer. Stop glorifying the flesh.

The panic that America is experiencing is because so many have built their house on sand and not on the rock. You can commit idolatry by glorifying a pastor, and you can commit idolatry by glorifying a politician. I greatly respect our president for many of his policies, especially as it relates to Israel. It is astonishing what he has accomplished.

But I want to add a warning. I have sat in Trump's rallies horrified as people idolize him almost to the point of worship, including many believers. All idols are coming down. I have seen pastors so drunk on power that they have prostituted themselves. They are running out at every opportunity to defend Donald Trump. Listen, Donald Trump is flesh, I am flesh, your pastor is flesh. No flesh can glory in His presence. All flesh is flesh. I want you to see this in Ezekiel 38:20. He declares, ". . .all the people on the face of the earth will tremble at my presence. The mountains will be overturned, the cliffs will crumble and every wall will fall to the ground."

The walls we put up to keep us from seeing the face of God, He is pulling all them down. The apostle Peter wrote, "The end of all things is near. Therefore be alert and of sober mind so that you may pray" (1 Peter 4:7). In Greek, "sober" means to be calm, collected, to have good sense, good judgment, or to be level-headed in times of distress. That is what we have been born to do. The Spirit of God is saying to be sober. Don't trust in the flesh. Seek the face of God and love Him passionately.

RETURN TO YOUR FIRST LOVE

America has an epidemic of backslidden churches pastored by backslidden pastors drunk on their own wine, obsessed with success and numbers that refuse to preach repentance or the cross. You know how you can tell? Ask yourself one question: When was the last time your pastor stood up in the pulpit crying and trembling and saying, "I need to repent"? God showed me something recently. *I* need to repent and be sober and pray.

Years ago, we had something called "praying through." You know, people don't do that anymore. They just pray. They walk up to the front of a church and say a few words and that's it. They are not really praying through. They are not staying on their face until the breakthrough comes, the burden lifts, and the glory falls. During the coronavirus, God has led me to slow down and pray four, six, and even eight hours that have sometimes seemed like only minutes. God has allowed this virus to pull the idols down, to call us into repentance, to stop running, and to humble ourselves before the Lord.

God is shutting down our busyness and our business, because flesh has been on the throne of our lives and chaos has been the norm. Everything is programmed in our churches—the songs, the sermon—there's not even room for the Spirit. The Spirit is saying, the rains, the floods, and the winds will not knock down the house that is built on the rock. The house Jesus is building is intimacy with Christ. This includes a Spirit-filled prayer life, a passion for the Word of God, and for souls. Repentance is the stone that will withstand the storms.

Yes, many Christians don't read their Bible. I've marked up more Bibles then I can name. They don't read that Word. They don't have a secret place with God on their face. Why? Because it's not vogue. It's not popular. It's not celebrated on social media. Are you panic stricken, filled with fear, obsessed with the latest news of COVID 19? That's an indication of a backslidden heart.

Hebrews 12:26-27 teaches, "Once more I shake not only the earth but also the heavens. . . .so that what cannot be shaken may remain." God is going to shake everything in sight so that He alone is savored.

The Lord is the only unshakeable power, both for believers and unbelievers. Are you ready for some good news? A great awakening is coming. Divine interruption is coming. The Lord has said to me, Jesus is coming for a glorious church, not a limping, broken, panic-stricken church hoarding toilet paper.

THE COMING AWAKENING

There have been two Great Awakenings in America. The First Great Awakening happened in the 1730s-1740s among a backslidden church. The pilgrims came here hungry for the Lord, hungry for the Word, and hungry for prayer, but their children lost the vision and became secular. Within a century, the fire of God had cooled in their hearts. The children of those immigrants wanted wealth and comfortable living. They were not hungry to repent and humble themselves. They wanted liturgy.

The same spiritual malice could be found throughout the American colonies. Philosophy, enlightenment, and education rather than repentance and intercession. Yet God moved mightily through people like George Whitefield, who spent hours bathing everything in prayer. The Spirit of God took over the nation. It was an incredible, astonishing miracle. Do you know what happened after that Great Awakening? The American Revolution (1765-1783). God saw what was going to happen and He sent an outpouring for the storm.

The Second Great Awakening happened from about 1790 to 1840. It was so powerful that one of the students at Yale University wrote home that, "The whole school is praying and praising God." You had Jonathan Edwards preaching about sinners in the hands of an angry God. It shook the nation. It was a Great Awakening that moved everything aside. What happened after that outpouring? The Civil War (1861-1865).

How does this relate to us today? Peter prophesied in Acts 3:19-20: "Repent, then, and turn to God, so that your sins may be wiped out, that times of refreshing may come from the Lord, and that he may send the Messiah, who has been appointed for you—even Jesus." Notice, the first word is repent. There is going to be a move of repentance and an outpouring of the presence of the Lord.

Second, God is going to send the Messiah, who has been appointed for you—even Jesus. We don't know when Jesus will return, but we do now the Lord has already come and made a way for us to live by the power of His Spirit. This world can't stop you if you are on your face in prayer and live focused on the Word of God.

God is going to send a third Great Awakening that is going to shake America and the world out of this coronavirus. Ezekiel 14:3 says, "Son of man, these men have set up idols in their hearts and put wicked stumbling blocks before their faces. Should I let them inquire of me at all?" Revelation 9:20 adds, "The rest of mankind who were not killed by these plagues still did not repent of the work of their hands; they did not stop worshiping demons, and idols of gold, silver, bronze, stone and wood—idols that cannot see or hear or walk." God must remove our idols before He sends revival.

King Nebuchadnezzar built a gold idol 90 feet tall and nine feet wide in Babylon. His leaders shouted for the people to bow down and worship it. Anyone who refused was to be thrown into blazing fire. In verse 12, three Jews named Shadrach, Meshach, and Abednego, refused.

The king was angry and threatened to kill these three godly men. How did they respond? Daniel 3:16-18 reveals their response:

> King Nebuchadnezzar, we do not need to defend ourselves before you in this matter. If we are thrown into the blazing furnace, the God we serve is able to deliver us from it, and he will deliver us from Your Majesty's hand. But even if he does not, we want you to know, Your Majesty, that we will not serve your gods or worship the image of gold you have set up."

Those three men were walking with the Lord, filled with His Spirit. Yet the king commanded the furnace to be heated seven times hotter, so that the flames killed the soldiers who threw them into the furnace. But then we read in Daniel 3:24-27:

> Then King Nebuchadnezzar leaped to his feet in amazement and asked his advisers, "Weren't there three men that we tied up and threw into the fire?"
>
> They replied, "Certainly, Your Majesty."
>
> He said, "Look! I see four men walking around in the

fire, unbound and unharmed, and the fourth looks like a son of the gods."

Nebuchadnezzar then approached the opening of the blazing furnace and shouted, "Shadrach, Meshach and Abednego, servants of the Most High God, come out! Come here!"

So Shadrach, Meshach and Abednego came out of the fire, and the satraps, prefects, governors and royal advisers crowded around them. They saw that the fire had not harmed their bodies, nor was a hair of their heads singed; their robes were not scorched, and there was no smell of fire on them.

Even the ungodly king recognized there is no God who can rescue like this. God is raising up fireproof believers who refuse to worship idols. Who will smile in the face of the fire? A Great Awakening is coming. But as David Wilkerson said, it's coming through repentance and it is going to begin in the pulpits of America. It is going to shake the world. Isaiah 26:20 declares, "Go, my people, enter your rooms and shut the doors behind you; hide yourselves for a little while until his wrath has passed."

2

HUNGERING FOR GOD

THE DRIVING PASSION of our hearts must be to know Jesus fully and allow Him to live His life through us according to His purpose, not our own. We hunger for God, wanting to say with all sincerity to a lost and dying world, "I've been with Jesus." It is only being with Jesus that will qualify us for the last great visitation that takes us beyond anything we have ever experienced.

As Christians, we have experienced glimpses of Christ's ministry unhindered, but except for a few occasional revivals, we haven't seen an outpouring of God's power as on the Day of Pentecost since Pentecost! The life of Christ within us is much larger than a random power surge, and the final great work of God will be much bigger than isolated incidents. Ordinary Christians are about to experience the unbelievable, behold the unthinkable, and witness book of Acts miracles.

STOP LOOKING AT THE SKY

The apostle Paul turned the fleshly Roman Empire upside down. He did not fight with fleshly weapons of war, such as legalism, pride, arrogance, and unbridled passions, but operated within the present-day ministry of Christ.

Our works will be judged as precious jewels, or as wood, hay and stubble. Instead of "a glorious church without spot or wrinkle," we will have a wedding dress that is dirty, wrinkled, and torn, worn by a bride with no sense of shame, who is still ignorantly anticipating the wedding with great enthusiasm. When our wood, hay, or stubble is burned, we may find ourselves knee-deep in ashes for our contemporary exaltation of flesh.

We are so busy struggling to live the Christian life, we have little energy for outrage. "Lord, help," we cry. "Help us, Jesus!" The Bible says, "Because he himself suffered when he was tempted, he is able to help those who are being tempted" (Hebrews 2:18).

If Christ *is* helping, why are so many Christians living through such hellish circumstances? If Christ is helping, why are so many backsliding and leaving the faith? If Christ is helping, why are thousands of churches closing each year in America?

"Why do you stand here looking into the sky?" the angels asked those who had gathered to watch Jesus' ascension (Acts 1:11). It's time that God delivers us from "heaven-gazers." Gazers pollute the purposes of God because they look at the sky, but live by their own agendas. They short-circuit the power of God in thinking Christ is "up

34

there, somewhere" because their only motivation is to empower the flesh. If Christ empowers gazers with "self" on the throne, He would make a mockery of the sacrifice He made at Calvary. The refusal to surrender complete control of our lives to Christ is a blatant declaration of war against His Lordship.

I missed it in the 1980s when I served on the executive committee of "Washington for Jesus" with Pat Robertson, Paul Crouch, and a half-dozen other evangelical leaders. We thought we could bring about a spiritual awakening to America by instilling Christian values in government. I also served on the executive committee for the American Coalition for Traditional Values with Jerry Falwell and Tim LaHaye. We worked with 110,000 churches, believing we could help. But we missed it; simply missed it.

The White House is not the key to revival—the church house is! Jesus does not reside in the White House. Jesus resides in the body of believers, *His* body. When the apostle Paul spoke of marriage as a union between a man and his wife, he said: "This is a great mystery: but I speak concerning Christ and the church" (Ephesians 5:32). There is a spiritual union and an ignition point; a Spirit-to-spirit contact between Christ and His church that births the manifestation of God's glory.

The Azusa Street revival led by William Seymour is considered one of the most significant events of the 20th century. Seymour reflected, "We wonder why sinners are not being converted, and why the church is always making improvements, and failing to do the work that Christ has called her to do. It is because men have taken the place of Christ and His Holy Spirit."

Instead of shutting ourselves in with Jesus, we run to meetings. We listen to this person who is anointed, or that person who hears from God, or this video our friends told us about, or that event we saw advertised. We rejoice over everyone else's victories and may even experience some of our own. But the Scripture says we are to become "more than conquerors" (Romans 8:37). We just don't continually experience the more than conquerors lifestyle ourselves. It's time to stop *talking* about doing His stuff and start *doing* it.

GOD, WILL YOU USE ME?

"God, I'm hungry. I want to know You. Will you use me?" Such were my prayers in Jerusalem on February 17, 1993, when God gave me a dramatic vision of a revival that would change the destiny of the world. It is not about a person, activities, or ideas. Christians have been obsessed with finding new ways to save face, or put on a new face, but the obsession of the believers who will usher in Christ's coming and reap the final harvest will be seeking *His* Face.

The vision God gave me contained very specific prophecies: Among them, the resignation of Boris Yeltsin before the year 2000. I was amazed on December 31, 1999, when news broadcasts interrupted New Years' celebrations worldwide with a special bulletin: "Boris Yeltsin in a surprise move, has stepped down and named his successor."

God showed me believers manifesting His glory in a greater way than the world has ever seen, with His power revealed until millions are called into the ministry. This power will be increased until believers will be filled up with the fullness of God.

God showed me a river of revival springing up in America by an unknown evangelist and pastor. This revival is the first fruit, a foreshadowing of a move of God greater than any revival, empowering His body of believers, the church, to release Christ in His present-day ministry and ultimately usher in the second coming of Christ. God showed me this final movement will be marked by greater intimacy between Jesus and believers, and a river of repentance, resulting in millions of souls coming into the kingdom. Hallelujah!

God wants to send a mighty fire today to burn up fleshly arrogance, to make His saints combustible, saturated with the oil of the Holy Spirit, lit on fire for the glory of God and mobilized for battle. In the book of Acts, pastors and evangelists weren't the ministers. Everyone who named Jesus Christ as Lord was a minister of the gospel, a flame for God. God wants to pour that kind of anointing out today, so there will be no big I and little you."

What must we do to be empowered to fulfill Christ's mission on earth?

GOD, WHERE ARE YOU?

Pray for the peace of Jerusalem. (Psalms 122:6)

After sixty-one days of fasting and prayer, God spoke the vision for the Jerusalem Prayer Team into my heart. This was to be God's dream, and God's team. After I heard from heaven, I flew to Jerusalem to meet with then Mayor Ehud Olmert to share the vision of the Jerusalem Prayer Team. He was greatly touched, and flew to Dallas in June 2002 to inaugurate this prayer movement. Dr. Franklin Graham, Dr. Jerry Falwell, Israeli Prime Minister Benjamin Netanyahu, Representative Dick Armey, and Governor Rick Perry were some of those who participated either by letter or video.

Christians from all over America and around the world have joined the Jerusalem Prayer Team. Many are household names, such as the the late Dr. Tim LaHaye Dr. Pat Robertson, Mr. Bill McCartney, Dr. John Maxwell, Mr. Pat Boone, Ms. Kay Arthur, Dr. Jerry Falwell, Rev. Tommy Tenny, and over 300 national leaders in America and thousands worldwide.

September 11, 2001 was a tragic day in American history. It was a physical manifestation of a battle that had been lost weeks, months, and possibly years before, because of a lack of prayer. Osama bin Laden had verbally attacked America for years, but the church was asleep. The demonic powers that were influencing him needed to be violently confronted by holy angels on assignment through the power of prayer—as in the time of Daniel.

I am certain God has raised up Nehemiahs and Esthers to do just that.

Today the Jerusalem Prayer Team consists of tens of millions of intercessors praying daily for national revival according to

2 Chronicles 7:14. It was King David who declared: "Pray for the peace of Jerusalem; they shall prosper that love thee" (Psalm 122:6). Praying for the peace of Jerusalem is not praying for stones or dirt. They don't weep or bleed. It is praying for God's protection over the lives of the citizens of Jerusalem. It is praying for revival. It is praying for God's grace to be poured out on the Bible land and all over the Middle East—prayer that demonic powers will be defeated by holy angels in a battle that cannot be seen with the natural eye.

The pastor of Corrie ten Boom's grandfather went to him and told him that his church was going to pray for the peace of Jerusalem. It inspired the ten Boom family to begin praying weekly. As Chairman of the Board of Corrie ten Boom House in Haarlem, Holland, we made the decision to revive this 100-year-old prayer tradition. Today, more than 73 million people are connected with us on the Jerusalem Prayer Team Facebook page, making it the largest religious social media destination in the world.

God has a destiny for you with us. Would you become a Jerusalem Prayer Team at Facebook.com/JerusalemPrayerTeam, and would you encourage others to do so? You can also join our email updates at JerusalemPrayerTeam.org or write to: The Jerusalem Prayer Team, P.O. Box 30000 Phoenix, AZ 85046.

The House of Israel is in a state of terror, as are all the children of the Bible land. They need the Lord to answer them in their day of terror. They need the God of Jacob to defend them. They need help from the sanctuary, and strength out of Zion. Now you know my personal prayer, and when it began.

The Corrie ten Boom House in Haarlem, Holland is the center for the Jerusalem Prayer Team in that nation. From there, churches of all nations are being encouraged to pray for the peace of Jerusalem.

Corrie would say to the Jews in the hiding place, "Don't worry, angels are around this house. You may not see them, but they are there, protecting you." Not one Jewish person the ten Boom family protected was caught . . . even the ones in the hiding place escaped after the Nazis came to arrest the ten Boom family.

Over the years, a great number of Jews were hidden in the clock shop, many for just a few days as they headed for Palestine to escape Hitler's ovens. When the Gestapo (the German secret police) raided the house, the entire ten Boom family was taken prisoner.

> It was the last time the ten Boom family would be together . . . Opa, his children, and one grandson. One hundred years before, almost to the day, in 1844, his father had started a prayer group for the peace of Jerusalem. And now, here they were, arrested for Judenhilfe, helping Jewish people escape Nazi persecution and death.[1]

---

1   (*Return to the Hiding Place*, Hans Poley, p. 147. Mr. Poley was the first person hidden by the ten Boom family.)

Casper (84), Betsie (59), and Christiaan (24) died as prisoners. Corrie suffered through prison, but by miraculous intervention, lived to tell the story. Four Jews who were hidden in the hiding place were never caught. They miraculously escaped to safety. Even though the Nazis knew they were there, they couldn't find them.

One of the four was a Jewish rabbi who vowed he would come back, and sing the praises of God. On June 28, 1942, the ten Boom family took him into their home. His name was Meijer Mossel. He was the cantor of the Jewish community in Amsterdam. He told the ten Boom's, "I am a chazzen (cantor). Where is my Torah? Where is my Shul (synagogue)? Where is my congregation? The goyim (Gentiles) have laid it all to waste. They have come for the Children of Zion! My only purpose in life is to sing praises to Adonai, the Lord. I am a Yehude, a Yid (one who praises Adonai.)"

In March 1974, he went to Corrie ten Boom's room, and with tears of joy streaming down his face, sang to the Almighty in Hebrew. The rabbi's life had been saved through the power of prayer. To his amazement, Corrie walked into the clock shop. As he walked downstairs, Corrie stood smiling at Meijer. She had just returned from the filming of the Billy Graham movie, *The Hiding Place*.

For approximately 100 years, from 1844 to 1944, the ten Booms conducted meetings to "pray for the peace of Jerusalem." It is amazing that God would tell me all those years ago to restore the clock shop. To think that the Lord finally got through my thick skull that prayer, and *only* prayer, is the key.

Mother Teresa was one of the first people to tell me in Rome that she would pray daily for the peace of Jerusalem according to Psalms 122:6. She said to me, "Love is not something you say, it's something you do." I believe that with all my heart. That is why I am appealing to you to join me in seeing what King David saw, what Solomon saw, and what our beloved Lord saw as they prayed in Jerusalem. Each experienced the power of God in Jerusalem—God's glory filled the house where they stood!

> "At that time Michael shall stand up,
> The great prince who stands watch over the sons of
> your people;
> And there shall be a time of trouble,
> Such as never was since there was a nation,
> Even to that time.
> And at that time your people shall be delivered,
> Everyone who is found written in the book.
> "And many of those who sleep in the dust of the earth
> shall awake,
> Some to everlasting life,
> Some to shame and everlasting contempt.
> *"Those who are wise shall shine*
> *Like the brightness of the firmament,*
> *And those who turn many to righteousness*
> *Like the stars forever and ever."*

But you, Daniel, shut up the words, and seal the book
until the time of the end; many shall run to and fro,
and knowledge shall increase."
(Daniel 12:1–4, NKJV)

Behold, the nations are as a drop in a bucket,
And are counted as the small dust on the scales; . . .
All nations before Him are as nothing,
And they are counted by Him less than nothing and
worthless. . . .
Even the youths shall faint and be weary,
And the young men shall utterly fall,
But those who wait on the LORD
Shall renew their strength;
They shall mount up with wings like eagles,
They shall run and not be weary,
They shall walk and not faint.
(Isaiah 40:15, 17, 30-31, NKJV)

THE GREAT AWAKENING

When we know Jesus, are known by Jesus and are abiding in Him, we fully understand the source, purpose and reason for which we were created; the hope of all our happiness, and the end of all our destinies.

Christ planned Pentecost. The inauguration of Pentecost was certainly more significant than a presidential inauguration. The strategic battle plan of Pentecost was designed in heaven to transform the world, and it did. On that day, 3,000 received the Word and were baptized. The Bible tells us that, "With great power the apostles continued to testify to the resurrection of the Lord Jesus. And God's grace was so powerfully at work in them all" (Acts 4:33).

Today's outpouring of God's Spirit carries the same spiritual significance as the original (Joel 2:23; Hosea 6:3; Zechariah 10:1; James 5:7). Multitudes will call upon the name of the Lord and be gloriously saved (Joel 2:32; Acts 2:21, 3:19 and Romans 10:13). This mighty world revival will include the house of Israel, and amount to the greatest Jewish awakening in the history of the world (Ezekiel 20:43-44; Jeremiah 31:34; Romans 11:24-26; Hosea 6:1-2; Amos 9:11-15 and Revelation 7:1-17).

"Ask ye of the LORD rain in the time of the latter rain" (Zechariah 10:1, KJV), said the Old Testament prophet. Hosea 10:12 states: "It is time to seek the Lord until He come and rain righteousness upon us" (see also Joel 2:17 and Acts 1:14).

In preparation for Christ's imminent birth and ministry, God planned that the world would have interconnecting, straight Roman roads and a rebuilt temple. Today, He is preparing for Christ's return by preparing Himself "a glorious church without spot or wrinkle" (Ephesians 5:27), filled with powerful believers who manifest Christ's ministry on earth. The sooner we admit our spots and wrinkles, the quicker we can fuse with who He is. Your perspective of Christ and His Kingdom will determine the possibilities you pursue.

God is preparing us for the greatest move in history, which will usher in the Lord's return. In this move, our churches will be packed on Sundays, and believers will be serving and fired up like never before. We will no longer be content with a lifestyle outside of the supernatural, but will be living an overcoming, victorious life in the realm of the Holy Spirit.

When Jesus begins to march, it is time for the church to move! God's last great awakening will plunder hell and populate heaven. Jews will be included in the most massive harvest of souls in the history of the world. Peter prophesied that there would be a mighty revival among the Jews, times of refreshing, that would come "from the presence of the Lord" (Acts 3:19). We are going to be changed from glory to glory. The spotlight of heaven will shine on hungry hearts. Those who thirst for righteousness will be filled.

We will no longer talk about God being manifested in spurts or seasons. Ordinary believers will so fully surrender to the life of Jesus in them, that He will reveal Himself in all His glory. All His prayers that have not been answered will be answered and manifested through us. We are about to see more than revival and more than a "move" of God's Spirit.

GOD IS PREPARING A HARVEST

A Christian content with status quo and business-as-usual comfort zones, living for "self" and bound by religious pride, will be cast aside when the Father chooses His workers for the end-time harvest. Those who are content to live without Christ on the throne of their life will miss the greatest, heavenly power-surge ever seen, empowering believers to reap a harvest.

Compromising Christians will be devoured in the final, end-time battle. The power they perceive they have will short-circuit as their dreams and visions putrefy like dead and rotten meat. We can't limit Jesus to our timetable; we have to get on His. God is not going to consult with us to determine His plan or purpose in our lives. It's our responsibility to determine if *we* are in *His* will, for He has made no provision to be in ours. We have not impacted the world because we have not been with Jesus. God is drawing the line, and sending angels on assignments to gather saints who are hungry and thirsty for Jesus.

This move will be a manifestation of the present-day ministry of Jesus Christ. It will not be a warmed-up or heightened sense of anything we currently see or do, but a surge of the power within us — the resurrection power that raised Christ from the dead — and through us, it will permeate the earth.

This unparalleled harvest will begin with a hunger to do the works of Christ. Believers who are tired of faking it and tired of making excuses for not fulfilling Christ's own words, will commit themselves to prayer and intimacy with Jesus. These believers will commit themselves and clearly see the person of the Holy Spirit. They will comprehend Christ's mission both in, and through them.

The motivation these believers have will be the same I

experienced when I was 11-years-old — a clear knowledge and understanding that we have a destiny in Christ!

In general, today's Christians have no such sense of destiny. But if we find out who the Christ is within us, we will be more excited about the Christian life than anything the world has to offer. Such enthusiasm kills inferiority, destroys the paralysis of the past, and gives a brilliant view of an open heaven.

In India, my daughter wept because of a leper with no arms or legs. I asked a doctor if they could cure leprosy. He explained that most lepers don't lose their fingers and toes due to injury, because they're desensitized to pain, but they can inadvertently rub them off. He said in previous years, the biggest problem was the rats chewing and eating the fingers and toes when the lepers went to sleep. A doctor found a cure. It was a "kitty cat." He tied a string around the leper and the other end of the string to the cat. When the rats came, the cat got the rats!

We have strapped to us the biggest cat, the Lion of the Tribe of Judah, to consume the enemy of our souls. He is in full battle gear and demons are trembling. He is clothed with the robe of righteousness and his eyes are as a flame of fire. He upholds all things by the word of His power (Hebrews 1:3).

When we become convinced that this Christ is in us, we will be a power that causes the enemies of the cross to quake and cower. America's Christian youth will be an indomitable force. All the false religious movements that ever existed will have nothing to offer our young people, when they understand *who* is abiding, dwelling and living in them.

When we're gripped with a sense of the destiny of Christ's mission and His present-day ministry, we will become "caught up" with seeing it operate in our lives. What moved us in our past will not move us in the present. We will become so caught up with a sense of direction and destiny, that we will do anything to please God.

Who on earth has a greater sense of destiny than the Lord Jesus Christ? Whose plan is greater than His? If He is going to release His present-day ministry through us, is there anything that could be more fulfilling? When we allow the "Lamb of God who takes away the sins of the world" to function through us, it will completely change our outlook.

CHANGE IS HERE

Staring us in the face is an eternal countdown that cannot be stopped. Every believer will have to make a choice to either live in God, or die. There will be no middle ground. Not to choose life will result in death by default.

To choose life is to seek after Christ with such zeal that little else matters, inviting the life of Christ to live in and through us, and allowing the power of Christ to fulfill His present-day ministry here on earth through us. We live when we allow the life of Christ to live in and through us to fulfill His present-day ministry.

"Their hearts will fail for fear" is the warning for these end-times. How could Christians' hearts fail for fear? Our hearts will if we haven't died to selfish pursuits, been with Christ, and shared His sense of destiny. Now it is time for God's blood-washed, Holy Spirit-filled children to come out of hiding and exalt Jesus as the King of kings and Lord of lords.

God is looking to see the life of His Son duplicated in our lives, to bring cataclysmic events into play through Spirit-to-spirit contact. The King of Glory is getting ready to shake us with the present-day ministry of Jesus Christ, which will ignite a generation of unborn destinies. This power surge will "short out" all our own ambitious, religious plans.

No longer will the destiny of the King be determined by our futile efforts. We will make no more attempts to protect or promote our own activities, but abdicate to the throne of heaven. The lost will then behold Christ. The Lamb of God will be made manifest in all His glory.

All of heaven will move as the power reserved for the Son of God will shine, blinding the powers of darkness. Armies will be subdued. The enemies of God will flee. The work of God, the final mission of the King of glory, will be seen and felt by all.

We have been served a sandwich of Christianity between sensuality and selfishness (Galatians 5:7). When we've been with Jesus in Spirit-to-spirit contact, self will no longer enter the picture. That man or woman, in just one day, will reap more fruit than in a lifetime

49

of attempting to live the Christian life with self-on-the-throne, filled with half-hearted intentions. The person of the Holy Spirit has made it possible. The fullness of Christ will be manifested through us, and we can truly be a people who have been with Jesus, like the saints of old.

David, in a spiritual awakening, danced into Jerusalem with the Ark of the Covenant (2 Samuel 6:12-23). Elijah on Mt. Carmel challenged the prophets of Baal, in a national awakening (1 Kings 18:1-46). John the Baptist declared, "Prepare ye the way of the Lord" and, "He will baptize you with the Holy Spirit and with fire" (in Matthew 3:1-12, KJV). We will have the white-hot fire of Christ's mission burning inside, shut up in our bones, so we can't help but speak it out and live it out.

CHRIST ABOVE ALL

The Bible says of the last days, "In that day will I raise up the tabernacle of David that is fallen" (Amos 9:11). Has the tabernacle of David fallen down? Yes, but in far more than a physical sense. King David had died. God wasn't speaking of King David. He was speaking of Christ, the *Ben David*, the son of David.

I am convinced that the tabernacle, which must be rebuilt before Christ's second coming, is a dwelling place for Christ, which is *not* just a physical tabernacle. The tabernacle of David has to do with *us*! We, our bodies, are the dwelling place for the Spirit of Christ. God is waiting for His children to take His Word literally and become the dwelling place, the tabernacle, for His Son in the most literal sense.

Peter commanded at Pentecost, "Repent, then, and turn to God, so that your sins may be wiped out, that times of refreshing may come from the Lord, and that he may send the Messiah, who has been appointed for you—even Jesus" (Acts 3:19-20).

The times of refreshing *are* coming, and Jesus Himself is going to be here, residing within our "tabernacles":

> Arise, shine, for your light has come,
>> and the glory of the LORD rises upon you.
> See, darkness covers the earth
>> and thick darkness is over the peoples,
> but the LORD rises upon you
>> and his glory appears over you.
> Nations will come to your light,
>> and kings to the brightness of
> your dawn (Isaiah 60:1-3).

The Lord appeared in an astounding vision to Isaiah and he saw the *kabod*, Christ's magnificent glory (Isaiah 6:1-4). The angels cried "holy" as Isaiah saw the Lord sitting high and lifted up on His throne. The posts were moving, God's train was filling the temple, and smoke was pouring out. Overwhelmed, Isaiah cried out:

> "Woe to me!" I cried. "I am ruined! For I am a man of

unclean lips, and I live among a people of unclean lips, and my eyes have seen the King, the LORD Almighty" (Isaiah 6:5).

We, like Isaiah, are unclean people in an unclean society, yet the glory of the Lord is ready to rise upon us, and nations will come to our light. All we have to do is allow Christ in!

Most of refuse to allow Christ to come in. We'll stand at the door of our lives and say, "Jesus, you can come into the living room, but don't touch anything." We keep Jesus out of the bedroom, out of the television room, out of our refrigerators, and certainly out of the kids' rooms. He built the house. He purchased the house. He is standing at the door ready to furnish the house with every good and pleasant thing, and we're running around seeing if we can tidy up enough of the house to allow Him to see a tiny part of it.

What are we denying Him access to when it's His dwelling place? It's like saying to the person who owns the home, "You can't come in. We can meet on the front porch, but I don't want you inside because you'll gain too much information, and gain access to the private parts of my life."

Where is Christ's dwelling place going to be? We must say, "Here You are, Lord, You can come in and do whatever You want. I'll surrender my own thoughts about what You should do and I'll do whatever You do, with You. I won't hinder You!"

The greatest manifestation of God's glory, power, and presence is going to hit this world through the kind of intimacy with Jesus that provides a place in which He can dwell. Just as my soul has my body for its dwelling place, so Christ, by His Holy Spirit, wants my whole body and soul as His dwelling place to control completely. The world believes a sinner can be demon-possessed. Yearn for the day that the world sees God's church Christ-focused.

CHRIST'S KINGDOM IS COMING

Jesus said, "Truly I tell you, some who are standing here will not taste death before they see that the kingdom of God has come with power" (Mark 9:1). What did He mean? Everyone who heard Him say that died physically. But many of them did see His kingdom come. They experienced the fullness of His present-day ministry within themselves.

Peter saw Christ's kingdom come, and people were healed just by his shadow falling on them. Paul saw Christ's kingdom come, and people were healed when pieces of his clothing were placed on them. John saw Christ's kingdom come in the midst of a prison island, surrounded by the worst elements of society, when he was caught up in a vision of the end-times seeing Jesus in all His royal, heavenly power. They saw Christ's ministry fulfilled on this earth.

Western culture has softened us, causing us to settle for a comfortable what's-in-it-for-me style of Christianity, rather than being willing to sacrifice for Christ, and paying any price to have His power and presence. I was once in the office of a presidential candidate who had publicly proclaimed his faith in Christ. I asked him what his political stance would be on the "hot" issues in Christianity, like abortion.

"The way you win elections is to avoid those black-and-white issues," he responded. "Abortion is really a non-issue."

"But why?" I asked in consternation.

"Because our polls show that as many Christians have abortions as non-Christians. In fact, there is little difference in the polls between people in the church and those outside it."

How sad. The church doesn't "vote its conscience" because its conscience is guilty! We haven't died to our flesh to allow Christ's holiness to be seen in our lives.

"Holiness" is treated in the church today as a throwback to legalistic, "hellfire-and-brimstone" preachers. We grew tired of them because we found the life they preached impossible to attain. Yet God repeatedly says: "Ye shall be holy: for I the Lord your God am holy" (see, for example, Leviticus 11:44-45 KJV, 19:2, 20:7-26, 21:8 and 22:32). Paul also issued a call for holiness (1 Thessalonians 4:7; 5:23). We shun holiness because we cannot live it and mock those who claim to be holy as self-righteous. We've blamed the holy life itself, rather than striving for holiness in our own lives.

Twenty-eight civilizations have come-and-gone. Ministries have come-and-gone. Visions have come-and-gone. Leaders have come-and-gone. No matter how powerful each was in their own right, they're now gone! Will our generation also just come-and-go?

Let's get onboard with what God is doing, so when He does it, we are not left behind. We must pray for Christ's mission to be accomplished. Joshua said, "Consecrate yourselves, for tomorrow the LORD will do amazing things among you" (Joshua 3:5). We need a pure understanding of Christ in us, and prayer to complete His mission.

If we are the salt and the light of the earth, why has the world invaded the church? Have we been vaccinated with a mild case of Christianity to protect us from the real thing? Evangelist Ray Comfort says, "Easy salvations have provided inoculations against Christianity." When the next Christian tries to witness to them, they say, "I tried that," as if Christ were a method to quit smoking, a medical treatment or a trendy diet.

We preach the cross, but for Christ's present-day ministry to operate in our lives, we must camp out at Calvary. We must invite the convicting power of the Holy Spirit into our lives, and let God's house, ourselves, become a "house of prayer." John the Baptist said: "He must become greater; I must become less" (John 3:30). This is not the current focus of believers, the concept of decreasing themselves. We keep increasing ourselves, our visibility, and our personalities through self-promotion.

God wants to do today what He did two thousand years ago. He has a final blow to execute. The first great battle was at Calvary; the last great battle is at the end-of-the-age for the final harvest. This is the final blow, the final assault, and the finished work of the cross. This last strategic blow will render the demons of hell bound in chains, and bring in the greatest harvest of souls the world has ever known.

Christ is longing for us today to be intimate with Him, so that He can become fully functional and fully released in us, manifesting His schedule, purposes, power, passions, and purity to fulfill His mission on earth. The battle that will allow Christ to perform His last great blow against His enemies is being waged right now over humanity's exalted flesh.

We are to become "the measure of the stature of the fullness of Christ," but only with Christ fully functional in us (Ephesians 4:13).

CHRIST IS ON THE THRONE

Why are most churches so weak? Why do we have to train and urge Christians to witness to others, instead of having a compassionate life force that naturally flows from within us? Why is the prayer ministry at most churches usually the least attended of all gatherings?

Billions of people on earth are bound for damnation, while we spend millions to strengthen the church in America. Yet we as a church sit week-after-week, unchanged because we do not have a vision of our true destiny in Christ. We don't understand what the life of Christ within us can accomplish, so we fall back confidently on our human works and are powerless against God's enemies. Jesus won't subjugate billions to hell while we are playing and not praying.

We must gain a profound sense of the mission of Christ who dwells within us.

Christ has a plan to fulfill His ministry through us. The Pharisees didn't get it. Religious Pharisees today still don't get it. They want to box in the Holy Spirit and conduct end-time ministry in their own way.

Look at where Christ is now. Isaiah saw Him sitting on the throne. Jesus is sitting while billions of people desperately need to hear His voice. He's sitting while pornography plagues our homes and churches. He's sitting while nations across the world continue to condone slavery and sex trafficking.

This Christ who does battle against spiritual powers, is sitting! Why? Christ is sitting because we're supposed to be standing! Christ has decreed and delegated the fulfillment of this ministry to us. He's sitting because He's the King and He's waiting for us to rise up as His army, armed and dangerous.

When you've truly been with Jesus, your passions forever change. Christ has a plan to empower His bride beyond anything the world has ever seen. Mighty men and women will be modern-day "John the Baptists." There is a world of difference between knowing about Christ, and having a personal encounter with Christ. There is a world of difference between trying to live the Christian life, and having Christ live His life through us. Religion gives us existence; Jesus gives us destiny. The flesh gives us today; the Spirit gives us eternity. In Christ, we understand the very source, purpose, and reason for which we were created, the hope of all of our happiness and the fulfillment of our destiny.

AS CHRIST REACHES THROUGH US, HE SPEAKS THROUGH US

Men and women who have wrestled with Jesus always trigger a heavenly response to their prayers. You and I have a date with destiny. Angels are waiting for assignments. It's time we make a God-connection and allow God to turn on the full blast of His fire in our lives. Our families, communities, churches, and nation are hopeless without a visitation from Jesus. There is no hope in a dead religion, in a Hindu cow, or a Buddhist temple, but there is great hope through the person of Jesus and a people who have been with Him.

God has promised He would move heaven and earth for those in pursuit of Him. He did just that at Calvary. A blast of eternity is shaking the earth so strongly, that even sincere Christians, who are trying to live the Christian life, without surrendering control, will be devastated by darkness. They will find themselves in their own sheltered bunkers, facing a roar of human agony with no power. Christ will reach out through us when we have been with Him.

It's time for the mouth of hell to experience the steel punch of God by people who have been with Jesus. In spite of the doctrines of devils and the philosophies of fools, scoffing at the cross and the blood, the Lord of glory will have the final word on this planet.

Only one thing will allow Satan to disqualify us to be part of the greatest move of God in history, and that is the refusal to dethrone self. Once we die to self, we will make a God-connection. The natural will encounter the supernatural and hell will be shaken. Worry will be a thing of the past because we will see our problems from our position in Jesus. We will be part of a generation that sees a great awakening.

3

·············

SEEING WITH SPIRITUAL EYES

FOR A CHRISTIAN, truth is not in the eye of the beholder
but is based on the Word of God. However, our perception of what is
happening in our life can affect our faith—and determine how we will
respond. When it comes to life's challenges, people often ask, "What's
happening?" There is a difference between what we see and what is
really taking place. Many Christians are simply afraid to face reality,
so they rely on their interpretation of the facts. But as a child of God,
we are called to walk in truth and light.

A good example of perception versus truth is found in the book
of Daniel. After spending nearly 70 years in captivity, away from their
homeland, the people of Israel had their perception of things, but
God revealed a deeper reality to Daniel. When faced with calamity or
confusion, it is easy to look at things from experience and miss the big
picture. As believers, we must never forget that even in our darkest

times, God is at work and He has a plan. We might not always perceive it, but reality is not always what we see.

THE SON OF DAVID

A prime example of the conflict between perception and reality is found in the Gospels. The story of Bartimaeus involves a blind beggar and it is the last of the healing miracles recorded by Mark:

> Then they came to Jericho. As Jesus and his disciples, together with a large crowd, were leaving the city, a blind man, Bartimaeus (which means "son of Timaeus"), was sitting by the roadside begging (Mark 10:46-47).

This man made an unusual pronouncement declaring that Jesus was the "Son of David." In other words, Bartimaeus acknowledged that Jesus was and is the kingly Messiah through his lineage with David. Isn't it amazing that the man who was blind could see who He was, but those who were the experts of the Law and Scriptures could not see Jesus as the Son of David?

A GARMENT OF BONDAGE

Not everyone agreed with his remarks. Mark 10:48-50 reveals:

> Many rebuked him and told him to be quiet, but he shouted all the more, "Son of David, have mercy on me!"
>
> Jesus stopped and said, "Call him."
>
> So they called to the blind man, "Cheer up! On your

feet! He's calling you." Throwing his cloak aside, he jumped to his feet and came to Jesus.

Bartimaeus was a beggar. There were three common areas where beggars could be found: at the gate of the temple, at holy rivers or springs, and on the highway or public thoroughfare. Historians tell us beggars carried a garment that identified a person's condition, which qualified a person to plead for financial assistance or would tell what type of ailment or disease they might carry. Depending upon the handicap, the article of clothing would depict what type of beggar he was. In this case, Bartimaeus was blind and could not wear ordinary clothing.

In addition, blind people were not allowed to remove their garment unless they were no longer handicapped or diseased. The longer they wore the garment, the more it became a stronghold of bondage in their lives.

CAST IT OFF

To outsiders, Bartimaeus' garment showed he was a man without the blessings of God. The reaction to his cry affirmed this position as the people attempted to silence him. But the Bible says the blind man cast off his garment, not *after* he was healed, but *before*. He cast it off to be healed. This was an important act of faith. In order to live free of fear and what others think about you, you must be willing to cast off what labels you.

Do not look at what's going on around you. Do not develop an attitude that is limited by the here and now. Commit yourself to a God who knows what is really happening in your life and cast off your blind man's garment. Bartimaeus cast off his garment when he heard the word from Jesus.

Cast off the lies that prevent you from seeing the truth about yourself, as revealed in God's Word. The mercy of God is far greater than your sin or your own inaccurate self-image. You can learn from your past. Let God show you the truth about your past, and His purpose for you in each circumstance.

The abuse I suffered, the rejection I felt, the fear, and low self-esteem from my childhood could have scarred me for the rest of my life. Instead, I have chosen to look at life with "kingdom eyes" and see Jesus through it all!

ACKNOWLEDGE YOUR NEED

Who was Bartimaeus, anyway? He was a homeless man with nothing to live for and no purpose. Can you imagine the scene Mark described long ago? Something happened to the blind man. Amid all the shouting and despite the heat and dust, the blind man heard a noise. Anything, a cart tipping over, or people bartering over the price of oranges could have caused the noise. But that was not what was happening.

Bartimaeus could have lost the miracle of his healing if he had been concerned with what others thought of him. Notice, Jesus did not go to him—Bartimaeus had to call out to Jesus. Not just once, but repeatedly, before he got a response. He had to persist, despite the crowd's warning for him to be quiet. Bartimaeus could have said, "If I am supposed to be healed, then Jesus will come to me. If He is the Messiah, then He will notice me." But that's not what happened. If he had focused on his circumstances, it would have destroyed his faith. Bartimaeus was helpless, not hopeless!

The Bible says that he was in desperate need. When you have a need, it is time to take action. Don't let Jesus pass you by when you need Him. Stand up and cast off what is hindering you and cry out to God!

LOOK TOWARD HEAVEN

Bartimaeus did not let his blindness dictate what he "saw." He turned his eyes toward heaven. He was looking for a miracle. If your eyes are accustomed to the darkness, it is natural that you will expect to see darkness wherever you try to look. When you look with faith, blind eyes are opened.

As Bartimaeus began to cry out, other people reprimanded him, trying to silence his voice. The religious leaders scornfully rebuked him. They probably wanted to test Jesus to see if He could prove He was really the Messiah. They wanted to see Him perform, but they did not believe He was really the King of kings and Lord of lords. Bartimaeus was willing to be humiliated and scolded by the entire town if that meant Jesus would stop and meet him at his point of need.

In your need today, whether it is a financial need, a physical healing, emotional restoration, or a miracle in your home, the devil will say to you, "Shut up! God will not hear you. Can't you see what is going on? Jesus is too busy. He doesn't care about you." Don't be fooled by the lies of the devil! Bartimaeus said, "Have mercy on me." In essence, he was saying, "Jesus, I am not focusing on what's going on around me. I am focusing on You."

KINGDOM EYES ARE BETTER

If you read Hebrews, you will see one word more than any other, "better." Hebrews says you are a *better* person than the high priest, a *better* covenant, a *better* sacrifice, a *better* promise. God's grace and mercy were not based upon Bartimaeus' condition, nor were they based upon his sin. Jesus responded in grace and mercy when Bartimaeus cast off his garment and presented his need to the Lord. Bartimaeus touched the heart of God and God touched the life of Bartimaeus.

The grace of God enables you to receive and empowers you to live as He desires you to live. Many people have the mistaken idea that God hates sinners and loves the righteous. Yet, exactly the opposite is true. God loves sinners and despises self-righteousness. When a person pronounces defeat, Jesus pronounces victory. This happens only when you can see through "kingdom eyes."

The Bible relates that when the Hebrew baby boys in Egypt

had been given the death sentence in Exodus. A mother knew that her little baby, Moses, was also doomed to die. But she had a promise from God. Instead of letting fear paralyze her, she looked at her circumstances from God's perspective. She laid her baby in a basket and set it adrift in the Nile. It must have been difficult to watch her son float away in the river in her little basket, but somehow she believed he would be safe. He was, after all, in God's hands.

That baby was Moses, who would grow up to become the deliverer who led Israel out of Egyptian bondage. Through Moses' leadership, the people of Israel witnessed glorious miracles. His faithfulness sparked the faith of men like Caleb and Joshua, who eventually led the Israelites into the promised land. An entire nation was changed because one woman dared to look beyond her circumstances and see with kingdom eyes.

When the angel Gabriel came to Mary and declared she would become pregnant with the Son of God, she said, "Be it unto me according to thy Word" (Luke 1:38, KJV). Others probably said, "We know what is going on here, Mary. You are an immoral woman. You should be stoned to death." They did not see with kingdom eyes.

When King Herod heard that the King of kings had been born, he tried to kill all the Jewish baby boys two years old and under. Herod was threatened by the birth of Jesus. He too did not see with kingdom eyes, and because of his fear, many innocent children were murdered.

GOD IS FAITHFUL

The book of Esther discusses Haman, a man who wanted to kill all the Jews. He plotted a plan of destruction through deceit and lies, and convinced the king to build gallows built for Mordecai and his family. He said, "The Jews are a growing nuisance. If I can kill Mordecai, I can kill the entire Jewish population, and my problem will be solved." He was convinced his plan would permit him to see that Mordecai would hang on the gallows.

What Haman did not know was that Queen Esther was a Jewish woman who knew how to see with kingdom eyes. Despite her initial fears, she interceded on Mordecai's behalf and his life was spared. As for Haman, he died on the gallows he had built for Mordecai! The Jews were delivered, because one woman dared to look past her circumstances and dared to set aside her personal comfort and safety. She dared to believe the Word and the promise of God. "And who knoweth whether thou art come to the kingdom for such a time as this." (Esther 4:14, KJV). From God's perspective, He had a plan even while the gallows were being built.

The Bible says David lived in the city of Ziklag, the city of despair. He was anointed to be king. Although he had killed the giant, Goliath, he still lived as a defeated man among his enemies. The Philistines had stolen everything David had, including his children and his wife. When everything looked bad, David encouraged himself in the Lord. He looked beyond his circumstances and saw God's faithfulness.

When you look at Jesus on the cross, you see two thieves beside Him. You see a man who was beaten and abandoned. You see the precious Savior, naked, humiliated, and scorned. Jesus had the power to call angels to stop the crucifixion, but He didn't. Why? Because He knew how to see with Kingdom eyes. He sacrificed His life and ministry, everything He had, so you could know Him as the truth. His definition of reality extends beyond mere circumstances; it is based on faith in a loving God who orders your steps and directs your path.

SALVATION SETTLED—ONCE FOR ALL

That day was a turning point for the entire world. The men and women who witnessed the brutality of the scourging and the horror of the crucifixion thought Jesus' life was finished. It wasn't. Jesus' work was finished, but not His plan. His life pointed to the cross, to His victory over sin, death, and hell. His loving sacrifice and glorious resurrection guaranteed our salvation is settled once and for all.

Where are you today? Are you living in fear and defeat because of your circumstances? Or, are you looking past those circumstances to see with Kingdom eyes? What is God saying through your circumstances? Here are three simple steps to follow when you think all is lost and there is no way out:

1. *Acknowledge God as your source.* If Bartimaeus had made anything other than God his source, he would have become bitter and barren. He wouldn't have had his need met. The

first thing the devil will do when you are in need is make a list of everyone who could help you but won't. God is your source!

2. *Maintain your joy.* Bartimaeus had plenty of reasons to not have joy, but he trusted the Lord and found abundant joy and new vision.

3. *Keep looking toward heaven.* If Bartimaeus had become distracted by everything that was going on around him, he would never have received his miracle. But his eyes were turned heavenward. Something in his spirit moved him and he focused his attention on heaven. He saw his situation from God's perspective and there he received hope and healing.

The Bible says in Mark 10:51-52:

"What do you want me to do for you?" Jesus asked him.

The blind man said, "Rabbi, I want to see."

"Go," said Jesus, "your faith has healed you." Immediately he received his sight and followed Jesus along the road.

"Along the road" implies that he became a disciple of Jesus Christ. He was more than grateful for this act of mercy. He took the next steps and submitted his life to Jesus. When you see life with kingdom eyes, you must act upon it with faith. Do not hold back. Do not let fear dictate your future. Pursue God and follow Him all the way.

DEAL WITH THE REAL

To be used by God, your priorities must be focused more on the spirit realm than the natural realm. Life in Jesus and in His Word is the only reality—everything else is superficial. The Bible says, "One night the Lord spoke to Paul in a vision: 'Do not be afraid; keep on speaking, do not be silent'" (Acts 18:9). What do these words have to do with faith—and fear? God told Paul, "Do not be afraid; keep on speaking," as though speaking would disarm the fear.

When people are fearful, they tend to speak according to what they see. When overwhelmed by circumstances, many focus on the negative and lose their hope. Fear, like faith, grows according to your words. If you speak out of fear, you will become more fearful. If, however, you confess your faith in God, despite your circumstances, you will be encouraged and find your faith stronger than ever. God wants us to deal with the real—life in Jesus that transforms us into people of the kingdom—not with surface realities.

A THOUSAND NEEDLES

When my son, Michael, was just a boy, he ran into the house one day, upset and overcome with fear based upon a fabricated threat from his sister. "Rachie said she was going to stick a thousand needles in my eye!" he cried.

I said, "Son, you will never see the day that happens."

"You better believe it," he answered, "because when there are a thousand needles in my eye, I won't be seeing at all!"

Some people live as though they have a thousand needles in their eye. They hear about kingdom reality, but they really do not believe it works. They do not see God's reality in their own lives, so they make excuses. They let fear keep them from living by faith. What about you? Do you dismiss people who are doing great things for God because you do not see His reality in your life?

You are no less important to God than your pastor or any other leader. St. Augustine said, "God loves each one of us as if there was only one of us to love."[2] God has called you to do great things in Jesus' name, but you won't fulfill that calling unless you get into faith and out of fear.

Living in fear is like living near a poisoned stream. If you drink from it, for the moment it will quench your thirst, but the result is death. Some people think fear is an effective motivator, but fear doesn't motivate anyone to grow, spiritually or otherwise. It only leads to deeper deception and greater bondage.

Throughout your life, you will deal constantly with two spirits—faith and fear. With faith comes power and with fear comes paralysis. The Bible describes many individuals who were conquerors in life.

---

2   http://en.wikiquote.org/wiki/Augustine_of_Hippo

They fulfilled their destiny and influenced the world because they spoke the truth—God's truth—and were not afraid.

What do the words of your mouth reveal about you? Do they reflect your faith in God, or do they indicate your bondage to fear?

A LIGHT IN YOUR FACE

King David is a great example of a man who knew how to speak the Word and disarm fear. When confronted by a menacing giant named Goliath, he said, "The Lord is my light and my salvation. Whom shall I fear?" Like David, when confronted by giants in your own life, remember what David said,

The Bible tells us David hid in a cave as war raged about him and his foes pursued him relentlessly. But David took words from God and used them as weapons to conquer his fear. He overcame both his fear and his foes, and God blessed his faith.

Look at Paul. He faced many crises in his life. People verbally attacked him. Some even tried to kill him, yet he was not afraid. Why? Because he had confidence in God.

Have you ever read one of those self-help books written to build confidence? I have. I have read many of them over the years. I could not relate to those authors. They talked about developing self-confidence, but confidence in self is not what I needed. The Bible does not talk about self-confidence; it says you should put your confidence in God.

73

GOD'S ANOINTING

I have been asked many times, "How do you minister to world leaders?" It is not because of my actions; it is because of my anointing. I speak with them without intimidation because the Spirit of God is upon me. He puts the words in my mouth.

God is the one who gives you favor with leaders and governments. In my travels, I have met people of all races, in various levels of importance, from numerous lifestyles, who want to know one thing: how can an individual overcome fear? The Holy Spirit gives you opportunities to speak the truth in love, and with each opportunity He will give you the anointing you need to speak. He gives you the wisdom and the words that will minister life, but you must be willing to listen and obey.

You know, Paul should have been experienced major guilt. He had persecuted the church. He had arrested Christians. Why, then, did Paul become so dynamic? Why was he able to conquer fear and impact the world with his teachings? What is the difference between Paul and you? He just had a whole lot of Jesus, and he understood the importance of speaking the truth.

Paul saw reality from God's perspective, and he let that reality permeate every part of his life. He accepted whatever God said as truth, whether it was about himself, the church, the Jews, or the Gentiles.

We live in a world that is full of excuses. If you ask someone why they do not believe in the Word, they will tell you, "Someone disappointed me in the church," or, "The church is full of hypocrites." But let me tell you—Paul didn't put his trust in a person; he put his faith in God.

66 REASONS FOR SUCCESS

I can give you 66 reasons why you will succeed if you start speaking the Word of God—the 66 books of the Bible! What will you get from God without faith? Nothing. What are you doing about all your problems? Worrying? Is it helping? Of course not. Will complaining help? Not a chance.

Why don't you start speaking the Word of God into your situation? Write the Scriptures down and start confessing them. Reverse the curse by speaking the Word.

You must learn to deal with the real. If you have fear, deal with it. If God has given you an assignment, no matter what it is, do not quit. You cannot lose if you do not quit!

It does not matter how many reversals you have. What keeps people from success is their deterioration from faith into fear. So many people give up for silly reasons. They give up on their jobs, marriages, schools, children, churches, and even God. Why? Because of fear.

Jesus had the toughest assignment in the world, yet He never offered an excuse. He never said, "I just can't do this, God." Nothing and no one could keep Jesus from doing what He had been called to do. Jesus said, "What the Father says, I say. What the Father does, I do. If you have seen My Father, then you have seen Me." Jesus set an example for us.

GET DESPERATE

You may have heard of Joni Eareckson Tada who was once a champion diver. On a summer day in 1967, she dove into the Chesapeake Bay after misjudging the shallowness of the water and suffered a severe injury that paralyzed her from the neck down. From a natural point of view, she is severely limited. What can she do when she can't move a finger, an arm, or a leg?

Joni, a beautiful woman, got into the Word of God and started speaking the Word. She stopped feeling sorry for herself and blaming others. As a result, she has touched millions of lives. She learned to paint beautiful pictures by holding a paintbrush in her mouth. She has written dozens of books, recorded several music albums, starred in an autobiographical movie of her life, earned numerous honorary Doctorates, and won numerous awards.

Nothing seems to hold Joni back. She does more than most women who do not live in a wheelchair. Why? Because she was desperate enough to believe and act upon the Word of God and be filled with His power.

Who would have thought Franklin D. Roosevelt could become President of the United States while he was confined to a wheelchair? Whoever dreamed that Napoleon, an epileptic who suffered from frequent seizures, could conquer a continent?

Walt Disney dared to show his little cartoon to some business people and asked them to help finance his vision for an animated film. They thought his idea was ridiculous. "You're not an artist," they told him. "Besides, no one is going to want to see a story about a mouse; people don't even like mice!" But now the whole world knows Walt Disney and his creation: Mickey Mouse.

Whoever would have thought that Beethoven, who became totally deaf, could continue to write beautiful music? God often uses our limitations to reveal His unlimited power.

CATCH HIS VISION

God is asking you today, "What do you want to do with your life?" Get the vision He wants to give you and do not be afraid! Deal with your fear and allow Him to guide you each step of the way.

Years ago, I spent the day with some dear friends, Jim and Jeanne Rogers. Jeanne has had a dynamic ministry as a singer and praise leader. She has sung at conferences across the nation, taught music workshops, and appeared on television. But as a young woman, Jeanne felt the pain of rejection. Her mother was divorced two or three times and her father, an alcoholic, abandoned her when she was a baby. But today, people look at her and say, "What a marvelous lady and a wonderful singer!"

Look at Evangelist James Robison. When he was born, his mother put an ad in the newspaper asking for someone to raise him. A godly pastor and his wife took James into their home as a foster child and shared the love of God with him.

But the promise of a loving family didn't last. Throughout his childhood, James was shuffled between the foster home where he felt safe and the house where his mother lived. There, he faced poverty, rejection, and abuse by an alcoholic father.

Today, James Robison is one of the most dynamic Christian leaders of our generation. His organization, LIFE Outreach International, is bringing the life and love of Jesus to sick, starving, forgotten people across the globe. In southern Africa alone, LIFE Outreach is helping to feed tens of thousands of children every month—and seeing multitudes saved through the power of the gospel.

What happened to these people? By God's grace, they stopped feeling sorry for themselves. They faced their fear and put their faith in Jesus. They saw reality from God's perspective and allowed it to redefine their future. They believed He had His hand on their lives, and they trusted Him, no matter what their circumstances told them.

Stop making excuses. Being angry at the world for your misfortunes will get you nowhere. You need to say, "God, You have a plan for my life. Show me that plan, and help me fulfill the call You have on my life. I trust You, and I thank You for loving me."

4

TOUCHED BY THE LORD

WE NEED JESUS. We sing about how much we need Jesus. We pray, "Jesus help me, I need You." We've felt the arms of our Savior, heard Him speak to our hearts, and felt that we have been with Jesus. We've experienced the salvation, grace, forgiveness, and mercy of Jesus. Sometimes we've seen His miracles, or experienced His life bursting through our own.

Despite how we've felt, the miracles we've heard reported, the success we've seen on the mission fields, and the movements breaking out all around us, today a growing number of Christians intensely yearn to be with Jesus. It is no longer enough to receive a spiritual high at a service, if we then go back to living an ordinary life where the hordes of hell rob us in our everyday lives.

I've experienced what I can only describe as the touch of God in my life, events that were so spectacular I could never understand why they happened, until now. They always came when I had the least amount of confidence in myself, and it seemed God had intentionally exhausted me. In fact, that's exactly what needed to happen so I would learn to trust Him.

At these times, I would be completely dependent upon God, knowing I could do nothing in my own strength, stripped of all self-confidence. My desperate prayer would be, "God, if You don't do it, it can't be done." I had no idea that my desperate heart's cry was the fertile soil in which the glory of God could be manifested. Now, I see clearly that all the times Jesus moved in was when I moved out.

The vibrant relationship we have with Christ is far from the scheduled services and meetings. Jesus is Jesus all the time. Almost every miracle Jesus performed was an interruption in His schedule. He yearns to interrupt our schedule to be with us, and be duplicated in our lives, so we will do "greater things" with Him.

DIVINE DISAPPOINTMENTS

"Hold your head erect, Mr. Evans," the optometrist demanded as he examined my eyes. The more I tried, the more difficult it became. I realized my head was shaking uncontrollably because of neck tremors. Finally, the optometrist said, "Mr. Evans, you need to see a neurologist to find out what is wrong with your neck."

That admonition began eight years of trudging from one specialist to another. I must have seen scores of neurologists, orthopedic specialists, and others to determine the source of the muscle spasms in my neck that resulted in head tremors. Little did I know that I had a rare genetic neurological ailment called spasmodic torticollis dystonia.

The harder I tried to hold my head straight, the more difficult it became. The muscles pulled my neck and twisted my head. The only way I could hold my head erect was to press my chin down with my hand.

As months and years passed, it grew worse. At first, I tried denial, assuming it would get better after a few weeks. When that did not happen, depression followed as I realized the disease could result in total disability. It was, at the very least, humiliating, especially for a public speaker.

No matter what I did, tremors were my constant companion. I was told that I must have an emotional problem, or was perhaps experiencing a breakdown. Instead of reaching out for support, I attempted to fake it. In time, I developed tachycardia. In seconds, my heart would jump from 80 to 120 beats per minute, and would race for 10 to 20 minutes. I felt as if I were dying.

This led to panic attacks that would grip me at the most inopportune times. I was scheduled to preach in as many as twelve different churches. While in the pulpit, a panic attack would hit like an electrical shock. It was humiliating and depressing. I became so discouraged that I stopped preaching for fourteen months. I was 32 years old, and it looked like my ministry was over.

The more I looked in the mirror, the more distressed I became. I questioned why I couldn't be strong like other leaders. Little did I know that God wasn't asking me to be strong. He was asking me to allow Him to be the strength of my life. The more I thought about it, the more depression settled over me. Ultimately, I realized I needed to turn the entire situation over to Jesus. I got on my face in prayer, and sobbed as I poured my heart out to God. I prayed, "Lord, I look around and I'm distressed. I look within, and I'm depressed. But, I am going to look to Jesus, and be at rest."

Like David of old, I stood on the Word of God: "The Lord is the strength of my life, of whom shall I be afraid" (Psalm 27:1, KJV).

"Even though I walk through the valley of the shadow of death, I will fear no evil, for you are with me;" (Psalm 23:4).

"I sought the LORD, and he answered me; he delivered me from all my fears" (Psalm 34:4).

"You will not fear the terror of night, nor the arrow that flies by day. . ." (Psalm 91:3).

"For God hath not given us the spirit of fear; but of power, and of love, and of a sound mind" (2 Timothy 1:7, KJV).

During that period of time, I produced more television specials and wrote more books than at any other time in my life up to that point. As a matter of fact, it seemed that supernatural doors were opening for me to be a confidant to world leaders more than at any other time.

I truly understood what it meant to know Christ "in the fellowship of His suffering, and in the power of His resurrection" (Philippians 3:10, KJV). I had to reach out to Christ to complete me in areas that were lacking. He changed me into what I was not.

Doctors suggested that I find a support group to help me deal with this incurable disease. I was told I would be that way the rest of my life. The only "support group" I attended was daily prayer with the Father, Son, and Holy Spirit. (I am not opposed to support groups, but I could not accept the fact that I would be disabled the rest of my life.)

Eight years after the first diagnosis, I underwent an eight-and-a-half-hour surgery by one of the doctors who initially discovered the gene. The surgery completely stopped the neck spasms.

Approximately eight weeks after the surgery, I was in Saudi Arabia and Iraq during the Persian Gulf War to proclaim the gospel of Jesus Christ. As Paul said, "When I am weak, then I am strong" (2 Corinthians 12:10, KJV).

ALL ABOUT HIM

The great embarrassment I now face is that the remarkable part of these stories is not how greatly, or how often, God has manifested Himself through me, but how little He does and how rare are those precious times. I have hindered Him, too self-centered to understand that He was not blessing "me and my ministry." He was allowing me to take part in His ministry. I assumed that I had a gift of the Holy Spirit empowering me, when the truth was the person of Jesus Christ had simply found a way to work through me to glorify the Father.

We rarely dream we are the problem. In my mind, the only problem was the devil. Jesus had already defeated the devil. Now, His greatest problem in manifesting His ministry in my life is "me." My heart's desire, by the grace of God, is to live my remaining years not allowing "self" to take over the throne of my life, where Jesus should be Lord and King.

It's about Jesus walking, talking, speaking, touching, and fully manifesting Himself. This is precisely God's plan for our time. The Apostle Paul declared:

> "[I pray that] the eyes of your understanding being enlightened; that you may know what is the hope of His calling, what are the riches of the glory of His inheritance in the saints, and what is the exceeding greatness of His power toward us who believe, according to the working of His mighty power. . . . Till we all come to the unity of the faith and of the knowledge of the Son of God, to a perfect man, to the measure of the stature of the fullness of Christ" (Ephesians 1:18-19 and 4:13).

A perfect man! There is only one—Jesus. Attaining "the measure of the stature of the fullness of Christ" is not about preaching or singing, although these have a part. It's not about programs or plans. It's not even about ministries. It's about Jesus—all His glory and all His riches and all His majesty manifesting Himself as He chooses, where He chooses, and when He chooses. I want to know

Jesus as the disciples did, as the early church did. But how can we do it?

END THE ROLLER COASTER

Two-thousand-years ago, during the Jewish feast of Pentecost, God poured out His Spirit upon the earth in a powerful manifestation that changed the world. Jesus' ministry has continued since then as a "present-day ministry" through the lives of ordinary believers.

On the Day of Pentecost, Peter experienced a complete transformation. This man, who had experienced the highs and lows of life with the Lord, suddenly arose and spoke out, prophetically and boldly. 3,000 people were added to the kingdom of God that day.

Peter started out just like many of us. He knew Jesus. He experienced the love of Jesus. He believed upon Jesus and named Him as the Messiah. He personally experienced Jesus working in special ways, such as when Jesus walked on the water. Peter received the full forgiveness and grace of the Savior after He rose from the dead and appeared to him. Jesus blessed him; he ate and had fellowship with the Lord. Jesus took time to disciple Peter, and took a personal interest in him.

Still, all this was not enough. Peter made futile attempts at living a Christian life, but it was impossible to do in his own strength. No matter what he did, Peter was still Peter, trying to prevail with God by his abilities. His name alone did not qualify him to experience God's power in his life. Peter was embarrassed that he couldn't live up to the victorious Christian life taught by his Teacher. Then, he denied the Savior and felt like an outcast among the disciples. Peter was embarrassed to show himself in the city where he was known. However, on the Day of Pentecost, something happened that was personally earth-shaking, and through Peter and the other disciples, it shook the entire world.

Peter had seen Jesus after His Resurrection. Peter had known that Jesus was alive. But on the Day of Pentecost, Peter discovered Jesus working through him! This was more than a spiritual "high" that made him resolve to live his life in a better way. Peter was a changed man! This same Peter went into the city later and saw a man begging. "Look on me," he said.

Why did he draw attention to himself? Peter had been ashamed to show his face. Nothing had changed in Peter's life through those entire three years of living with Jesus. What was there to see in Peter? Peter knew that if the man looked, he would see Christ in him because Peter had become Christ's representation, fulfilling Christ's mission and ministry on earth. What was so different? Nothing, except Peter had been with Jesus and the life of Jesus was in Peter to glorify the Father.

Jesus has a present-day ministry. He is no longer on earth physically as a human, but His ministry continues in the lives of believers. Jesus lives in us through the power of the Spirit to continue His mission on the earth.

Christians today are being called to live out the present-day ministry of Jesus Christ. The present-day ministry of Jesus Christ is Jesus living completely through the believer unhindered, in the person of the Holy Spirit, so He can fulfill His purposes on a daily, hourly, and moment-by-moment basis. Jesus fulfilled His ministry through the early church in the life of Peter and other believers, and they turned the world upside-down!

"Greater things will you do than I have done," Jesus told His disciples. We are yearning to see this today. We want to see Jesus' plans fulfilled and His prayers answered. I take the liberty to deviate from the traditional term for "revival," and define it as a supernatural work within the church and also within the world: a supernatural salvation and a great awakening.

JESUS CONTINUES TO WORK TODAY

I've seen and experienced the unhindered work of Christ. How it happened and why, I did not understand until later. That's where I discovered these truths.

I am the least likely "qualified" to bring them to you. I grew up in an abusive home. Because of my mother's Jewish heritage and teaching, I was brutalized by a "Christian" father. At age four, I started running away from home. I remember the police once bringing me back, where I was quickly locked in the canning closet for punishment. There, I prayed my first prayer with a broken, hungry heart.

At age six, I was a stuttering, dysfunctional, and wrecked little boy. Yet, inexplicably, I remember the date of an important decision I made that year. On September 12, while playing in a park in the early evening, a group from the nearby nursing home came out to feed the pigeons. With tubes and bottles dangling around their wheelchairs, they held pieces of bread in their shriveled hands and threw them to the pigeons. They offered some to me, but I threw it down and ran home crying, "I don't want to feed the pigeons!" Without conscious awareness, I had a divine discontentment that shrank at the thought of living my whole life without any sense of meaning, simply inhaling and exhaling and ending up in some park feeding the pigeons.

Those precious people in my mind's eye are symbolic of Christians we've seen grow old around us. How heartbreaking to think we could end up with only "birdfeed" to show for our lives! I see that wrecked little boy as symbolic of what many of us are spiritually. Stuttering in our efforts, dysfunctional in relationships, illiterate in the things of God, yet unwilling to live that way, we stumble through life.

We should realize that if we do what we've done in the past, in the future we'll have what we had. I don't want that for my life. I understand that it is time to wrestle with God because I want the fire of God to consume me. I want Jesus to live in all His glory through me, to speak through me, to love through me, and to reach through me. It's not about me—it's about He! It's about the King of kings and Lord of lords having full control in my life, and yours.

It wasn't until Jesus appeared to me at age 11 that a ray of God's light entered my life. It was my first experience of intimacy with Jesus, even though I didn't know what it meant in all its fullness. After a stint in the military and determined to live for Him, I attended a Bible college. Anything I knew about Christians had come from my Catholic community in Massachusetts. When I arrived at the Bible school, I'll never forget asking, "Where do we pick up our robes?"

At age nineteen, I began preaching the gospel. For 32 years, I worked as hard as I possibly could to reach the lost, from the marble halls of the United States government to the hellholes of the world. When I would see God's favor, I thought God was blessing my ministry. I didn't understand He was really blessing His. And I saw it only inconsistently. I sometimes experienced the supernatural, but I couldn't maintain supernatural living. I never dreamed that God could offer so much more for our lives.

The Gospel of Luke describes a woman who brought an alabaster box of ointment to anoint Jesus as He visited the home of a Pharisee named Simon. The woman wept, and washed His feet with her tears while wiping them with her hair, kissing His feet and anointing them with oil. Some rebuked her, but Jesus said: "You didn't give me a kiss and yet, this woman has not ceased from kissing me. You didn't anoint my head with oil. This woman has anointed my feet."

This is the same Christ who is reaching out to us today. This response is the spirit that turns the head of God and moves the hand of God, the spirit of humility and brokenness.

THE REAL PROBLEM

We are hindered when self, instead of Christ, is on the throne of our lives. This is why the divorce rate in the church is rising reflects the divorce rate outside of the church. This is why young people leave the church, focused on entertainment or career. We try sincerely, but we don't seem to realize we are sincerely "trying" to live the Christian life in our own strength. We retain our "self," our own interests and concerns, as the center of our life. Yes, we strive to be good Christians, but who really gets the final word when the pressure is on? Is it Christ in us, or just us?

Although I continued struggling for over three decades to be the best father, husband, and Christian possible, I failed. I failed because I was attempting to live up to a standard I could never achieve. No one can. Christ and only Christ can live that standard, and He lives it through us. When He does, we then know the meaning of "the measure of the stature of the fullness of Christ" and we see God's glorious promises manifested in our lives. The world then sees that we have been with Jesus.

We cannot win in the natural what Christ has won at Calvary. All attempts to do so are paramount to treason. When we claim to be able to live the Christ-life ourselves, without Christ on the throne of our lives, we attempt to compete with Calvary. Instead of a "great awakening," we will experience a "rude awakening" if we don't repent!

Until our hearts are surrendered to the Lord, fully and completely, self will only attempt to put Band-Aids on festering sores. The wonderful reality is that Christ has already won the battle. When you and I realize it's about "He" and not about "me," God will reign triumphant in our lives.

5

ROLLING AWAY THE STONE

MANY YEARS AGO, I prayed at the tomb of Jesus in Jerusalem. A sign there reads, "He is not here—He is risen" and hangs on the door of the empty tomb. Mark 16:1-3 says, "When the Sabbath was over, Mary Magdalene, Mary the mother of James, and Salome bought spices so that they might go to anoint Jesus' body. Very early on the first day of the week, just after sunrise, they were on their way to the tomb and they asked each other, 'Who will roll the stone away from the entrance of the tomb?'"

Verse 4 says that the stone "was very large." Who could roll away a stone that weighed several thousand pounds? Yet, the next two verses tell us the stone was already moved when the two women arrived. "But when they looked up, they saw that the stone, which was very large, had been rolled away. As they entered the tomb, they saw a young man dressed in a white robe sitting on the right side, and they were alarmed."

In verse 9, Jesus makes His first appearance. "When Jesus rose early on the first day of the week, he appeared first to Mary Magdalene, out of whom he had driven seven demons." Isn't it amazing that Jesus would appear first to Mary Magdalene, a former prostitute who had been transformed into a woman of great faith?

Imagine yourself in Jerusalem. It's Sunday morning, the first day of the week. Your Lord has been brutally killed and buried. Your dreams for the future have been shattered. Then you hear that the huge stone has been rolled away by the power of the Holy Spirit. Would you believe it? Is the truth of it a reality in your life today?

Like Jesus' followers, many Christians want to hang on to the stone. There are stones in your life that God wants to roll away—if only you will make Him your source.

THE PROBLEM WITH STONES

For 4,000 years, the Jewish people have had serious problems with stones. I made this statement to the Russian Jews who had converted to Christianity when I was preaching in Israel one time. When these Jewish Christians came into the country, the government stuck them in the most desolate places, but they came from everywhere to hear the Word of God.

I reminded them that God told Abraham to leave his country and go into the promised land. In Genesis 15:7, He said He would give

Abraham the land. "You have left your country and gone into the promised land," I told them, "and God has promised to bless those who bless thee."

Isaac woke up one morning, ready to inherit the blessing of Abraham. Later, when he had received the promise, he went to check out all that was supposed to be his, but it did not look very promising. The enemy had put stones in the wells, and there was no water. Without water, everything dies. It becomes desolate. The Bible says, "With joy you will draw water from the wells of salvation" (Isaiah 12:3). Just as Isaac had to get the stones out of the wells to get to the water, you have to get the stones out of your life so they don't block the flow of Jesus in you.

JESUS IS ALIVE!

On resurrection morning, a living Christ rose from the dead to roll all the stones away, but those who did not acknowledge God as their Source were still in defeat.

Jesus was risen. He was Lord. He was alive! Mark 16:14 says that when Mary Magdalene told his disciples that Jesus was alive, they did not believe her. "Afterward he appeared to the Eleven as they were eating; he rebuked them for their lack of faith and their stubborn refusal to believe those who had seen him after he had risen."

Many people today do not believe that Jesus is alive, but I have more faith in His existence than I have in your existence. When you make God your source and put your faith completely in Him, He will roll the stones of life away. Do not be among the shallow Christians who spend all their time asking God to fix their problems but avoid any real intimacy with Him. They want relief but not true release.

Jesus came so you could experience God full blast, so He could kick the walls of your life down, bind defeat and discouragement, and bring you true joy. The choice is yours. You can continue to face your problems by yourself, or you can allow Jesus to be your source.

THE KEYS TO HELL AND DEATH

How do you get the stones rolled out of your life? Believe that He is risen in your life. Arm yourself with His power and become dangerous to every spiritual force of evil you encounter.

Many people say, "I don't believe in being militant." Well, my Bible tells me about a mighty Lord who appeared to the apostle John on the Island of Patmos. In Revelation 1:17-18 (KJV), John said, "And when I saw him, I fell at his feet as dead. And he laid his right hand upon me, saying unto me, 'Fear not; I am the first and the last: I am he that liveth, and was dead; and behold, I am alive for evermore, Amen; and have the keys of hell and of death.'"

When you acknowledge God as your source, you have the keys to hell and death. You do not fear death, people, the past, the present, or anything the devil sends your way. You may be knocked down, but you will never be knocked out.

There are thousands of born again Russian Jews who live in Israel right now. They know God is their source—He led them there for a purpose. Actually, the state of Israel brought them in, not realizing that God, in His prophetic plan, would use them to evangelize the nation.

When we ministered to them years ago, it was the first meeting to be held in the nation since these Russian Jews had come together. I preached a message on the fire of God, because we were near Mt. Carmel where Elijah the prophet had called fire down from heaven. I said to them, "God has made you flames of fire." They believe in God as their Source; they know He can roll the stones away. Still today, they are experiencing spiritual awakening in tremendous ways.

Once you realize that Jesus has conquered death and the grave, that He has the keys to hell, and you acknowledge Him as your source, He puts faith in you and takes out fear. When faith operates in your life, the walls come down and the stones in your life are rolled away.

A GREAT AND MIGHTY WORK

Since I was on my way to Moscow, those Russian Jews gave me a letter to give to the Jews still living in the former Soviet countries.

It was a prophetic letter. They had posted it in their churches. It said, "Come home to the land of Israel. Come home according to the prophecies. The Lord is pouring out His Holy Spirit. Join us in this great end-time revival."

God is doing a great work on the earth. He is moving today in a mighty way. There is a huge printing press in Beijing, China. It is the press that former Chairman Mao Tse-tung used to print his infamous

Little Red Book. Years ago, the Chinese foreign minister signed a document, allowing the gospel of Jesus Christ to be printed. Now, millions of Bibles have been printed on this same printing press. Many of them have been loaded on trains and shipped to Russia. Think of it! Bibles coming from the same presses that Chairman Mao once used to print communist materials of death and doom now share Jesus with those in faraway lands. Today, China prints more Bibles than any nation in the world.

GOD IS MOVING

God is moving in a big way, a way that reminds us how near we are to the coming of Jesus Christ. When you think of the ongoing turmoil in the Middle East, you may say, "I don't know what is happening." Do you realize that many of our world's greatest revivals are taking place in some of these nations? Iran has been noted as the fastest-growing Christian nation.

There is a battle to be won, and God is not going to stop until all the stones are rolled away. He is in the stone-rolling business. All He needs is a stone—and faith—and He will do the rest.

He has spoiled principalities and powers before. Take heart! You can march big, shout big, and believe big! No matter what your problems are—whether financial, emotional, or relational problems, or circumstances beyond your control—they will be resolved if you give them to Jesus. Once upon a time, there was a dismal Friday, but Sunday was just around the corner. There *will* be a resurrection!

THE MESSIAH IS STILL AT WORK

One time, my wife and I flew to Holland where Corrie ten Boom lived. We went into her home, which we have now restored and made into a witness for the Lord. Hers is such an incredible story, and we knew it would touch the Jewish people.

While we were there for a meeting, it was Liberation Week in Holland. The country decided to spotlight the ten Boom clock shop and home as a symbol of liberation.

Holland is a country that did not permit the gospel to be proclaimed on its television stations at that time, yet they gave us two hours of prime time. The whole nation saw the movie *The Hiding Place*. The station then gave us time at the end of the broadcast to talk about Corrie ten Boom and the Jesus she knew. We were also on three national radio stations! Stones will be rolled away if you let God be your source.

Later, an 81-year-old woman came up to Carolyn and me and said, "I was twenty-three years old when they took me from my home and put me in a concentration camp. I did not know anything about Jesus or God except that I hated them. There were two girls on the bunk above me. One was Corrie, and the other was her sister, Betsie."

"Betsie was very ill. When the guards gave bread to them, Corrie and Betsie gave part of it to others and had communion. I listened to them singing songs. I turned to them and asked, 'How can you believe in God and Jesus when we are all going to die? How can you sing in this hellish place?'"

"Corrie looked at me and said, 'Because Jesus is alive.'"

That elderly woman gave her heart to Jesus Christ because of two women who refused to be defeated by the darkness of hell, but believed instead that Jesus is alive. She said, "I am alive today because of Corrie and Betsie ten Boom."

YOU WILL RECEIVE POWER

What happens when the stones are rolled away in your life? Acts 1:8 says, "But you will receive power when the Holy Spirit comes on you; and you will be my witnesses. . ." You may say, "I know all about Jesus," but that means nothing. Jesus hung on a cross, taking upon His own body your sins, so that you might have peace with God.

John 3:16-18 (KJV) says, "For God so loved the world that He gave His only begotten Son, that whosoever believeth in Him should not perish, but have everlasting life. For God sent not His son into the world to condemn the world; but that the world through him might be saved. He that believeth on him is not condemned." Revelation 3:20 says, "Behold, I stand at the door, and knock: if any man (or woman) hear my voice, and open the door, I will come in to him, and will sup with him and he with me."

Your perspective of yourself will determine the possibilities you pursue. When God is your source, you won't have a bad self-image.

No matter what the devil has done to you in the past, when you have resurrection life, the keys to hell and death, the power of the Holy Spirit, you will never see yourself as defeated.

You will pursue greatness because you serve a great God. Just as He turned Mary Magdalene into a woman of great faith, God turns captives into conquerors when the stones of life are rolled away.

FAITH WINS

Do you sometimes feel your needs exceed your supply? Do you run out of money before you run out of bills? Do you feel physically drained? Are you afraid of emotional bankruptcy? Do you feel like you are spiritually starving? Again, whatever your need, God is your source, and His provision is perfect.

1 Kings 17 shows how God brought a drought to the land of Israel to punish Ahab, the King of Israel, for his wickedness. The drought lasted for three and a half years, and it resulted in a great famine. Yet, despite the shortage of food and water, God took care of Elijah. He told the prophet, "And it shall be, that thou shalt drink of the brook; and I have commanded the ravens to feed thee there." (1 Kings 17:4, KJV).

God used birds to feed Elijah, and He supplied water from a small stream. If you are facing a famine in your life, take heart! God has not forgotten you! He will meet your needs, even if He has to use birds and brooks!

FAMINE IN THE LAND

The famine that hit Israel lasted a long time and was devastating. You may feel devastated by your circumstances today. You may have a serious shortage in your finances. You may feel pressured, worried, and upset. You may have unmet emotional needs, and as a result, you feel depressed and alone. You may be experiencing a physical setback through sickness, disease, mishap, or outright catastrophe. You can live in fear—or, you can turn your attention to the source.

When you have calamity in your life, you can do one of two things: You can turn to God and learn from the experience, or you can give in to fear, worry, and unbelief. If you permit fear and doubt to dominate your thinking in times of need, you will be unable to receive the provision God has for you. The dry period will escalate into a full-blown famine. You must be on guard during the dry times, or you will be overwhelmed by your own needs. When famine comes, you cannot talk yourself into joy, or bargain your way out of debt. Famine will drain you of your life, energy, hope, and even health.

Elijah's attitude was to focus on God's goodness and mercy, making the best of his situation and learning from this experience. He refused to let fear and unbelief dominate his thoughts. Instead, he was grateful to God. When there is a famine in the land, the Holy Spirit can assist you to demonstrate an attitude filled with gratitude, peace, and joy.

Elijah trusted God to meet all his needs and as a result, goodness, mercy, signs, wonders, and miracles followed. Elijah had faith that prevails. What about you? You can lose—or you can win. You can prevail—or you can fail. The choice is yours.

THE RAVENS WILL FEED YOU

As Elijah came to the brook, the Lord said, "I have commanded the ravens to feed thee there." Isn't it comforting to know that God can supply your needs? He is not affected by your circumstances. He is not limited by your problems. He does not have to use conventional methods to care for you. He can feed you with the help of ravens!

The Jews considered ravens to be unclean. They were dumb scavengers, fearful of men, yet God chose to feed Elijah with these very birds. Had Elijah been religious, he would have rejected the food from the ravens based upon the Law. Instead, he could discern the word of the Lord and know it was His will. This method seems to be a contradiction. But God uses methods we never think of. Ravens were scavengers and were selected because they are more daring to approach a crowd of people to steal food, than any other bird.

Incidentally, the king was probably the only one with meat, and had his butchers prepared meals for the king, the ravens would fly down and grab the meat. But what is even more amazing is that the ravens had to be controlled by the Spirit of God. For them to give away their bounty was against their nature. Elijah was being fed from the king's table and his source was God, not the ravens. If God did not manipulate nature, the ravens would never have turned themselves over to the prophet.

God will supply all your needs, but He may not do it in a way you expect. He might surprise you. He might tell the ravens to feed you!

That is all right. Receive His provision. Let the Holy Spirit guide you. Allow Him to meet your needs in the way He deems best.

DRY BROOKS

It seems Elijah was well cared for. The ravens brought him fresh bread and meat every morning and every night. He had cold, clean water to drink. He had everything he needed—until the brook dried up. Rain had not fallen, and the water eventually evaporated. As Elijah sat by the brook, he must have wondered why God had permitted his only source of water to vanish.

Do you ever feel like that? Do you wonder why you are spiritually dry, emotionally void, close to financial ruin, or weary and desolate? Sometimes, God allows you to go through dry periods so you will thirst for Him. Hosea 10:12 says, "Sow to yourselves in righteousness, reap in mercy; break up your fallow ground: for it is time to seek the Lord, till he come and rain righteousness upon you."

Your "brook" may be completely dry, but that does not mean God has abandoned you. He is ready to meet your needs! He is happy to meet them! But you must seek Him.

As soon as the brook dried up, God told Elijah what to do next. In verse 9, He says, "Arise, get thee to Zarephath, which belongeth to Zidon, and dwell there: behold, I have commanded a widow woman there to sustain thee."

In the natural, that sounds crazy. "Now, son, I want you to go to the next town and knock on a stranger's door. Tell her you want to live in her house for a while. It will be all right. Trust Me." What would you do? Would you obey God, or would you let fear and embarrassment keep you from having your needs met?

Elijah chose to obey God. He did not care what anyone thought or said. He trusted the Lord, and God not only met his needs, He also used Elijah to save the life of the widow and her son.

Verses 12-15 says, "And she said, As the Lord thy God liveth, I have not a cake, but an handful of meal in a barrel, and a little oil in a cruse: and, behold, lam gathering two sticks, that I may go in and dress it for me and my son, that we may eat it, and die. And Elijah said unto her, Fear not; go and do as thou hast said: but make me thereof a little cake first, and bring it unto me, and after make for thee and for thy son. For thus saith the Lord God of Israel, The barrel of meal shall not waste, neither shall the cruse of oil fail, until the day that the Lord sendeth rain upon the earth. And she went and did according to the saying of Elijah: and she, and he, and her house, did eat many days."

THE WIDOW'S MIRACLE

Why did God allow the brook to dry up? I believe there were two reasons. First, He was giving Elijah an opportunity to obey His voice. Second, He knew the widow needed a miracle.

Elijah's willingness to do what the Lord asked allowed the Lord to demonstrate His provision for the prophet, and for the widow and her son. When God tells you to do something, remember this story.

He may want to use the occasion to meet not only your needs, but the needs of someone else as well.

Elijah stayed at the widow's house for some time, and God took care of the three of them. They had enough meal and oil to last through the famine. It was a great testimony to the people of her town, I'm sure.

Then, just when life was bearable again, tragedy struck. Verse 17 says, "And it came to pass after these things, that the son of the woman, the mistress of the house, fell sick; and his sickness was so sore, that there was no breath left in him." Imagine what she must have thought. "Here I have opened my house to a man of God. I have seen a miracle performed through the meal and oil. But now, my only son has died."

In verse 18, she said to Elijah, "What have I to do with thee, O thou man of God? art thou come unto me to call my sin to remembrance, and to slay my son?" How do you respond when tragedy strikes? Do you blame yourself? Do you blame God? Do you turn against God's people?

Verses 19-21 gives the prophet's answer, "And he said unto her, Give me thy son. And he took him out of her bosom, and carried him up into a loft, where he abode, and laid him upon his own bed. And he cried unto the Lord, and said, O Lord my God, hast thou also brought evil upon the widow with whom I sojourn, by slaying her son? And he stretched himself upon the child three times, and cried unto the

Lord, and said, O Lord my God, I pray thee, let this child's soul come into him again."

This was a terrible moment for Elijah. He had heard the voice of God and obeyed Him repeatedly. Despite his obedience, the widow's son fell sick and died. Life is not always easy for the people of God. Sometimes there are terrible moments when there is nothing you can do but cry out in desperation to God.

Several years ago, my oldest daughter gave birth to triplets and there were complications. They were born prematurely and we could have given in to fear. The situation was certainly serious enough. Instead, we cried out to the Lord. For several weeks, we prayed and sought God's face. We asked for mercy and healing, and God answered. He strengthened the babies so that they were able to go home.

God also heard Elijah's prayer and healed the widow's son. Verses 23 says, "And Elijah took the child, and brought him down out of the chamber into the house, and delivered him unto his mother: and Elijah said, See, thy son liveth." And the woman said to Elijah, "Now by this I know that thou art a man of God, and that the word of the Lord in thy mouth is truth."

God brought a dead child back to life, but He also brought new life to the widow's dead spirit. Prior to this experience, she had respect for God, but she did not know Him as her Lord. When she saw life return to the body of her little boy, something deep within her heart was stirred. For the first time, she knew the Word of God was true and worthy of her trust.

God is a God who gives and gives and gives and gives. He is a good God, and His generosity is the basis for the biblical principle of generosity in our own lives.

Have you ever told someone, "You're going to reap what you sow"? That statement is true. If you plant tomato seeds, you will harvest tomatoes. If you sow love, you will reap love. If you sow mercy, you will reap mercy. If you sow into the kingdom of God with your finances, He will bless you. Galatians 6:7-8 says, "Be not deceived; God is not mocked: for whatsoever a man soweth, that shall he also reap. For he that soweth to his flesh shall of the flesh reap corruption; but he that soweth to the Spirit shall of the Spirit reap life everlasting." This does not mean God will give us earthly riches when we give to a ministry. However, we store up riches in heaven as we follow's God's plan to show generosity to meet needs and support the ministry of the gospel.

In the beginning, the widow had to give Elijah the last bit of meal and oil she had; she had to sow her meager supplies to reap abundant provision from the Lord. In other words, she had to exercise her faith. Later, she had to turn her dead son over to the hands of a prophet to receive him back alive. She could have given up, but she did not; she chose to exercise her faith.

Had the widow refused to obey God, either by denying Elijah the last of her meal and oil or by refusing to give him her dead son, the result would have been death. By turning to God, she found life for herself and for her son—and faith that prevails.

How is God asking you to exercise your faith today? In what impossible situations is He asking you to demonstrate your trust? Are you sowing what you want to reap? Or, are you planting seeds of fear and doubt?

You will reap what you sow. If you are in need today, turn to the Lord. Trust Him to provide; then obey His voice. Exercise your faith in the name of Jesus. Give Him room to move in your life as He wills.

Then, plant seeds of mercy, patience, kindness, love, joy, and peace, and watch the Holy Spirit produce a rich harvest in your life— and in the lives of those around you.

THE PRAYER OF FAITH

Acts 12:1-17 (KJV) tells the story of Peter's arrest. Herod set about persecuting the church, and in the process killed James, the brother of John. Verse 3 says, "And because he saw it pleased the Jews, he proceeded further to take Peter also." He threw Peter in jail.

It was a dark time for God's people. Brutal Roman soldiers were hunting them, and one by one, their leaders were either killed or imprisoned. To their credit, the disciples asked the Lord to help Peter. Verse 5 says, ". . .prayer was made without ceasing of the church unto God for him."

They prayed all night. The only problem was that they were filled with unbelief. God miraculously released Peter, and when he knocked at the gate of the house where they were meeting, the disciples did not believe he was really there!

Verses 13-16 say, "And as Peter knocked at the door of the gate, a damsel came to hearken, named Rhoda. And when she knew Peter's voice, she opened not the gate for gladness, but ran in, and told how Peter stood before the gate. And they said unto her, Thou art mad. But she constantly affirmed that it was even so. Then said they, It is his angel. But Peter continued knocking: and when they had opened the door, and saw him, they were astonished."

Rhoda was so excited to hear Peter's voice; she did not stop to let him in. She just ran back and told the others. "Hey, guess what! Peter's here! That's right; he's just outside the gate!" They didn't believe her.

"No way," they said. "Peter's in jail. It must be his angel." It was only by the grace of God, and by Rhoda's persistence, that Peter was allowed to enter the house of his friends! When you pray, be ready to receive God's answer! Expect a miracle. Trust His Word, and allow Him to be God.

James 5:16 says, "Therefore confess you sins to each other and pray for each other so that you may be healed. The prayer of a righteous person is powerful and effective." Do not try to dictate how God should answer your prayers, or when. He knows what you need, and He knows the best way to meet your needs. Remember, He is a good God!

Mary, the mother of Jesus, said in Luke 1:38, "May your word to me be fulfilled." That is one of the most powerful statements a person could make. You will never accomplish all that God has for you unless you submit yourself to the Word of God. You can have prevailing faith; just acknowledge God as your source, and believe His Word.

WHEN NEEDS ARISE, RELEASE FAITH

Miracles rarely occur during times of plenty; they occur when your needs are greatest. The needs in your life will either prompt you to respond or react—you will either respond in faith to God, or react in frustration, fear, and anger for your circumstances.

Prevailing faith does not make rash judgments in times of need. Prevailing faith does not let anger dictate actions. It does not make demands. Prevailing faith rests in peace and joy, and allows God to move as He sees fit. Prevailing faith says, "God, You are my source, Your Word is true, and I believe it. It is settled, and I am going forward in the name of Jesus."

GOD AT WORK

I was speaking at a church in Little Rock, Arkansas, one time when I received a call about a young man named Randy Van Pay. My wife Carolyn called to tell me he had been injured in an car accident.

He was pulling out onto the road when a speeding car rammed into his. Randy's car was smashed, and he was thrown out.

His heart stopped three times before the EMTs got him to the hospital. His entire left side was crushed. One lung collapsed, and the other was barely functioning.

His parents called my wife and told her it looked like he was not going to make it. Carolyn immediately began to pray. As she did, God gave her a promise: "I will heal him and bring glory to the mourners."

I joined my wife and together, we fought for Randy in prayer. The next morning, Carolyn and I drove from Little Rock, to Orange, Texas, praying all the way. When we arrived, it was late, so we went straight to bed.

The next morning, I drove to the hospital. I said, "God, I thank you that Randy is healed. I see Randy healed. I believe that Randy is healed."

I walked into his room in the intensive care unit and saw him lying on the bed, with tubes running everywhere. Fluid was draining out of his lungs. He had several monitors attached.

"Randy Van Pay," I said.

He put his hand over his tracheotomy and said, "Yes?"

"You look wonderful. You are healed. Your head is healed. Your chest and lungs are healed. God has sent me here to tell you that you are totally healed, Randy."

"I am healed," Randy replied. He reached up and pulled the tubes out, and immediately, the machines went crazy. The hospital staff ran us out of his room. I am sure they thought we were dangerous fanatics.

Fifteen minutes later, a nurse came downstairs with big tears running down her face. She said, "I don't understand what happened. I just do not understand. Your friend is sitting in a chair outside the door of the ICU. His lungs are perfect. There is no fluid anywhere. His heart is working perfectly. There does not seem to be anything wrong with him. He is just sitting there, resting in a chair!"

I said, "There is nothing wrong. He has been healed."

PAST THE DROUGHT TO THE RIVER

You may be experiencing a dry time in your life right now. You may have cried out to God and asked why He has abandoned you. You may have complained about His lack of provision. You may have let fear and anger rule your heart and determine your course of action.

You may have faced tragedy, the death of a child, a divorce, financial failure, a crisis in your health. You may have despaired, even as the widow in 1 Kings 17 despaired.

But look up! God is still on the throne. He has not turned His back on you, not for one moment! He knows you are hurting, and He understands your anger and frustration, but He wants you to be healed in the name of Jesus. Experience a faith that prevails.

6

THE LORD IS YOUR STRENGTH

WHY DOES GOD RESIST the proud but give grace to the humble? Because the proud person does not ask for help—not even God's.

The shepherd boy of Bethlehem became the king of Israel of Jerusalem. David knew that when God fought for Israel, the Israelites won every battle! Sanctuary for the believer is in God's presence.

Where is His sanctuary? Now He resides in the believer.

David got more revelation about God, and from God, in the Psalms, than anyone else in the entire Bible, except our Lord. David was the most excited, enthusiastic, and dynamic worshiper in the entire Bible. It didn't happen by accident. David had to get his prayer answered in his time of trouble to break through into revelation and joy unspeakable, full of glory. David stepped out of rejection into revelation! He stepped out of depression into delight.

STEP OUT TO STEP UP

When you place your worries in the Lord's hands, you realize that it's not what you're going through that will determine your destiny and your disposition. It's God who determines your steps.

The greatest book of inspiration and encouragement ever written, the Psalms, was birthed out of the heart of a man who determined he would not live in self-pity, but would put his faith in the Lord in his times of terror, and trust God to answer his prayer. David could not sit around blaming others, waiting for life to be fair and others to fight his battles. He had to stand up like a warrior in the midst of adversity and encourage himself in the Lord.

David could not rely on others for his victory, and neither can we. As long as we are lethargic, indifferent, and lack responsibility, we will never fulfill our destiny. A warrior mentality does not exempt us from difficult circumstances, or even setbacks. It causes us to rise to a new height. It will cause us to realize that the past is dead, as God said to Joshua, "Moses My servant is dead. Now therefore, arise . . . Every place that the sole of your foot will tread upon I have given you, as I said to Moses" (Joshua 1:2-3, NKJV)

What has God promised you? Do you have a vision for victory for your life? If you will live by the promises of God, meditate on His Word, and determine that you will allow nothing to keep you from becoming everything God has created you to be, then you will, indeed, develop a warrior spirit. You will stand against the forces of darkness, look them squarely in the face, and encourage yourself in the Lord. David faced adversity and said, "I am going to pursue, overtake, and recover all" (see 1 Samuel 30:8). And so will you!

The Bible says, "The people that do know their God shall be strong, and do exploits." (Daniel 11:32, KJV) God did not choose King David to live in this end-time hour, but He has chosen you. Refuse defeat! Guard your words. Encourage yourself in the Lord. Remember that you are guaranteed victory from the creator of the universe because of what our Lord did at Calvary. You have to rise up and fight the fight of faith.

"In him we live and move and have our being" (Acts 17:28, NKJV). We reside in Him.

"Don't worry, Maureen, help is on the way!" As I turned, I thought, "What have I just said?" The lady was Maureen Reagan Revell. She and her husband Dennis had just returned from a fact-finding mission meeting with African presidents for her father, President Ronald Reagan. I had a dream to go to Africa and hold great crusades.

The Lord had told me to go to Mexico to the Princess Hotel in Acapulco and pray for two days. On the second day, I was outside praying when a couple walked by.

The Lord spoke to my spirit. "Ask her if you can help her resolve the president's great need in Africa."

"Lord, she doesn't know me, and I don't even know who she is," I said to the Lord. I didn't find out who the woman was until I told her what God had related to me. It was then that she introduced herself and her husband. She was Maureen Reagan. Well, I have learned that I can never win an argument with the Lord, so I obeyed and asked her if I could help her. Her response was one that I should have expected because of the God we serve.

"Yes, you can. There is a new president in Uganda. He wants to speak to U.S. broadcasters. I can't arrange a big meeting. Can you?" Maureen asked me.

"Yes, tell him help is on the way! I will call Dr. Ben Armstrong, the executive director of the National Religious Broadcasters, and ask him if he will allow President Museveni to speak."

Dr. Armstrong said "Yes." Later, what a joy it was for me to host President Museveni's cabinet in my suite at the Washington Hilton Hotel.

Museveni rededicated his life to Christ in that meeting and invited me to Uganda. His secretary of state became my crusade coordinator for Africa. God is amazing! When we trust Him instead of our human reasoning, great things can happen.

The flesh refuses to trust in God. Instead, the flesh life trusts in stuff, in people, and in self. David could say, "been there, done that—no thanks."

One time I sat in the Dallas-Fort Worth Airport waiting for my flight and I noticed a security guard. The Lord impressed me to speak to her.

I felt led to say, "Help is on the way," and to tell her, "She is blessed and highly favored and that God is not angry with her."

Tears streamed down her face as I shared the Word that the Lord had placed in my spirit.

She responded, "Mike, my mother just died. She was a godly woman, as was my grandmother. I rebelled against them. I have three children and no husband, no food or gifts for the kids for Christmas. But I told the Lord I would put Him first and two days later I got this job. I'm so grateful."

"Well," I said, "so am I." I handed her money to buy food and presents for her kids. She broke down crying with joy. She said, "I thought God was mad at me! That was a lie, wasn't it? Yes, it was. I will get in church Sunday."

"Where should I go?" she then asked me. After giving her some directions, I went on my way. She ran up to the plane and said, "God bless this man of God."

Do we need help? Do we need to be strengthened? Yes!

The root word for Jerusalem means "inheritance" or "estate." Our God desires to send us help and strengthen us from His abundant estate, and our inheritance through His shed blood.

Angels came straight from heaven's sanctuary to strengthen our Lord.

ONLY IN THE LORD'S STRENGTH

I have found that God intentionally allows us to exhaust ourselves when we are operating in our own strength. We must wake up and realize that only He can provide the strength we need.

One morning in prayer I heard the words in my spirit, "Go to Jerusalem. What you do will affect the destiny of the nation." I contacted 12 partners, told them what God had told me, and asked them to meet me there.

The night before they were to arrive I became greatly troubled.

"Lord, I don't know what we're here for. I can't tell these people I'm taking them on a tour. They really believe in me, and that you have sent us here for a divine purpose! What am I here to do?"

"Go to sleep," I sensed the Lord saying.

While I slept, I had a dream. I saw the man on a platform with me saying, "Thank you for coming. The reason we are here is. . ." and nothing came out of my mouth. I tried it again: "The reason we are here is . . ." and the same thing happened. It really shook me.

Finally, in the dream, I started for the door to get out of there. Suddenly I saw an angel as big as the door. He shouted, "The key to the mission is Zerubbabel 4:6." I awoke from my sleep.

Our group of 12 ended up in the house of Prime Minister Begin, praying over him. I asked everyone to join hands. Then we prayed for a general by the name of Sharon, who would later become Israel's prime minister. We prayed for many generals that week. Charles Duke, one of the Apollo mission astronauts, began weeping and asking forgiveness of an Israeli general.

Charles shared with the general that on a trip to the moon, he found Jesus Christ, and "He forgave me of all my sins. I was anti-Semitic and I must confess this to you and ask forgiveness."

The news broke 48 hours after I arrived home. The phone rang, and it was the senior advisor to the prime minister. "Mike, I have great news. War broke out in Lebanon, and we shot down 90 Russian MIGS and destroyed 2,500 SAM missiles without losing a plane. It is a miracle. Thank the men for coming and praying over our leaders. God has answered that prayer."

I hurried back and told the partners to turn to the book of Zerubbabel, the fourth chapter, the sixth verse. This verse was the key to the mission. Well, I'm sure you've figured it out—there is no book of Zerubbabel. I then said, "Men, I don't know what to do. I only know that the Lord said come." At that the angel shouted "Zechariah." I alone saw the angel and heard the words. I immediately turned to Zechariah 4 and began reading.

Then the angel woke me from my dream. He asked me, as if I had been asleep, "Do you know what you see?"

"No, I don't," I said.

He said to me, "This is the word of the LORD to Zerubbabel: 'Not by might nor by power, but by my Spirit,' says the LORD Almighty" (Zechariah 4:6).

HELP IS NEAR

No matter what you're going through, help is on the way—if you will put your trust in God's power. God really does understand where we are in our situations, circumstances, and trials. He sees our "black holes" of poverty, grief, abuse, neglect, unhappiness, and malaise in life.

At 19 years of age I was living in downtown Philadelphia. It was my last year in the Army, and the pay wasn't much, around $300 a month. I came into town after visiting my folks and parked my car in a parking garage. I gave the attendant an extra five-dollar tip to watch my car, and my stuff, especially my stuff.

Instead, someone stole everything I owned in the world. The car, my clothing, and everything else was gone. I didn't have money for food, so I fasted for a week while I stayed at the YMCA. Near the end of the week, I went to the Salvation Army. It was rough, especially since the next morning was Christmas. I walked to church in the snow. I only had $3.25 left when I went to a diner and ordered bacon and eggs. As I was reading my Bible, a Scripture jumped out at me: "No eye has seen, no ear has heard, no mind has conceived what God has prepared for those who love Him, but God has revealed it to us by His Spirit" (1 Corinthians 2:9-10).

I needed that Word. No, my circumstances did not change that day, but within one week eight miracles happened. Yes! Help was on the way. I needed to just get my flesh out of the way so God could show up in a big way.

David needed help all the time, and God sent him help. God wants to do the same for you, too. David returned home to Ziklag one day to find out that he had lost everything. All his family, everything was gone, taken by the Amalekites. His men were so angry that they wanted to kill David. But David knew that help was on the way, and he "strengthened himself in the LORD his God" (1 Samuel 30:6, NKJV).

David prayed, David worshiped, and he called on his priest Abiathar for counsel. He marched 600 of his men 15 miles to the brook Besor. 200 of the men stopped there because they were exhausted. The remaining 400 joined him to hunt the Amalekites enemies.

David related that he had found a half-dead Egyptian on the side of the road and had compassion on him, giving him food and water. The Egyptian had been left to die by the Amalekites, but David saved his life. The Egyptian knew where the enemy was and because of David's kindness gave David this invaluable information. David's men regained everything that the Amalekites had taken, and more.

The prayer of David is called a "Warrior's Psalm" to be prayed before going into battle—a prayer for victory in battle!

What battles do you need victory in? God is ready!

"David became greater [Hebrew = "a long stride"] and greater [Hebrew = "a large embrace"] for the LORD God of hosts was with him" (2 Samuel 5:10, NASB). When David prayed this prayer with all of his heart, he became God-defined, God-embraced, and God-saturated.

I was once scrubbing the pots with sand; it was my turn to do the dishes. In the desert you use sand, not water. Water is too precious to waste.

Everyone else was already asleep. Jamie Buckingham had given the devotion at dinner about the "church in the Sinai in the Old Testament." I had the mother of all headaches. Earlier that day we had been planning to climb Mt. Sinai, where Aaron had held Moses' hands up for victory in battle (see Exodus 17:12).

I decided I didn't want to spend hours going "slowly 'round the mountain," so I took off my shirt and extra gear and ran straight up. By the time the team arrived, I had heatstroke and was sick as a dog. Bill, an astronaut from Florida, was giving a devotion on being one in Christ. I badly wanted to get off the mountain. I tried to pretend I was fine until I knew I could not stand it any longer.

"Bill," I said, "I'm sick, dehydrated, and have sunstroke." He gave me water and a shirt and hat and helped me down the mountain. I was very embarrassed. As I thought about the day, I kept thinking what a stupid idea it had been to come on this trip.

"How can I get out of this desert of snakes and scorpions?" I asked myself.

Wind and heat! It was awful. As I was complaining to the Lord, I picked up my Bible and opened it to where it told about the children of Israel and their murmuring and complaining (see Exodus 16). The Lord asked me what was wrong. I admitted to the Lord that I was proud, stubborn, and rebellious. In addition, I didn't like to submit to authority! With that confession and admission of guilt, the Lord instantly forgave me, and my headache and fever left!

The next day we came up on a Bedouin tent. A panicked Arab woman heard that a doctor was in our team. Angus Sergeant was an internist. The woman brought her baby, who had an infection covering its entire head. The baby's head was matted with flies and green matter about one-half-inch thick. They had taken knives and burnt the baby's head, scarring her face, in trying to kill the infection. I thought Angus was our hope for the hour.

"I can't help. The infection has to come off. She needs surgery," Angus said. Suddenly I felt the compassion of our Lord for this little six-year-old girl. So I placed my big hand on the abscess and prayed in Hebrew.

I knew that the mother would understand some of the prayer because Hebrew and Arabic are very similar. Gib Jones, a professional photographer, took a picture. There was no sign of a change when we left.

The next morning Dr. Sergeant said, "I've got to operate on the little girl. I will do the best I can—otherwise she may not live." Angus was the first one in the tent. I waited outside. Three or four minutes passed, and then I heard him crying. I opened the flap. He held a dirty cup of tea in his hand. It was the best offering the poor Bedouin could give. He was crying as he lifted it up, saying, "Lord, this is the greatest physical miracle I have ever seen." The child was totally healed. "Nothing is left on her head and all the scars are gone. If you can heal this child you can keep whatever is in the cup from harming me." He swallowed it, rejoicing. I wept with him, blessing the Lord for allowing me to be a living sanctuary in the Sinai.

Yes. Help was on the way! I was the only thing hindering help's arrival. When I got out of the way Christ reached through me, and with a blast of glory healed that little girl.

There were times during David's desert experience that his life, like mine, must have seemed like an emotional roller coaster. Without the Lord becoming his light, and enlarging his darkness, David would never have fulfilled his heavenly assignment.

Late one evening on our trek up Mount Sinai, everyone began to stumble as darkness descended. "Turn off your lights," Jamie said. "Let the light of the stars guide you. Your eyes will adjust." We did, and panic hit me for a moment. Like David, I was out of my comfort zone. I wanted to trust in myself, but my eyes needed to adjust to the darkness. Within moments, millions of stars were glowing like fireflies, illuminating our path. How like us humans to try to create our own light, to focus on ourselves rather than on "The LORD. . .my light and my salvation" (Psalm 27:1, KJV).

TRAINING TIME

My heart's desire was to get as far away from my father as possible. The United States Army beckoned, and I ran. "How far can you send me?" I asked the recruiting officer.

"Korea," was his reply. And that's where I ended up, on a mountain called Wong Tong Nee. I was 17 years old, terrified and alone.

My first morning there, God gave me Psalms 5:2-3: "Hearken unto the voice of my cry, my King, and my God: for unto thee will I pray. My voice shalt thou hear in the morning, O LORD; in the morning will I direct my prayer unto thee, and will look up" (KJV). On top of that mountain in Korea, I gathered six big boulders and made a place of prayer. Every morning for 14 months I prayed on that spot.

Almost twenty years later, I was invited to preach for Dr. Cho. He looked startled when I told him about my prayer place on Wong Tong Nee and asked if I could go there to pray. When I arrived, there were literally thousands of people praying there. It had become none other than Dr. Cho's Prayer Mountain. A million and a half people go there every year to pray! It was there that I had prayed in 1964 and 1965. Dr. Cho bought it in 1966! I was the first person to pray on Prayer Mountain. I had thought I was running away, but instead I ran right into the loving arms of my Savior. I learned, like David, that sometimes Gods stills the storms; other times, He stills us in the midst of the storm (Psalm 107:29).

I went to Korea in a storm of fear and frustration. It was there that I learned that when you allow what God says to be the final word, you are stilled during your storm, even if the storm is still raging around you. I realized that God always provides a promise bigger than the problem and defeats the demons of darkness. When we put what God says above our circumstances, our faith in His Word becomes the "fragrance of heaven" that turns the head of God!

Just as I was sent to Korea in the midst of international turmoil, so David was sent to Sokoh. His assigned task was to deliver food to his brothers during a battle with the Philistines (1 Samuel 17).

As David approached the battlefield, he found himself in a battle, not between two armies, but between two men—Saul and Goliath.

Saul was bowing; Goliath was bragging. Saul was cowering; Goliath was cursing. Saul was praying; Goliath was primping.

Terror was the order of the day! Goliath was a descendant of the Anakim, the same giants who had struck fear into the hearts of the spies Moses had sent into Canaan some 400 years earlier. The rebellion in the ranks of the rescued had caused the children of Israel to wander in the desert for another 40 years before they entered the promised land.

Rebellion and discontent had again placed them in a valley of decision. Unhappy with God's plan, the people of Israel demanded to be ruled by a king—Saul—rather than the King of kings. Israel wanted to follow a proud king who refused to bend or bow and could not be broken. To their great regret, they received one in Saul. But God wanted the worship of a broken king who would gladly humble himself.

Although Saul stood head and shoulders above the men of Israel, he was no match for the real giant, fear. Like his ancestors before him, Saul felt like a grasshopper in the presence of Goliath. Leaders today are often selected by the same criteria by which Saul was chosen: a good head for business, broad shoulders to bear the burden of business, impressive good looks. David was chosen because he was a man who longed to know the heart of God.

It seems that Saul should have been the one to go into battle. The entire nation was trusting in him. After all, Saul looked like a king. He was trained. He had the armor. He was from the tribe of Benjamin, those experts with the slingshot! But a rock in the trembling hand of a fearful king would never find its mark. It would take pure, uncompromising faith in an awesome God.

Religious flesh often disguises itself in kingly robes that hide the profane, ungodly heart. Jesus bluntly charged the scribes and Pharisees: "Woe to you, teachers of the law and Pharisees, you hypocrites! You are like whitewashed tombs, which look beautiful on the outside but on the inside are full of dead men's bones and everything unclean" (Matthew 23:27). When the world does not see, and say, "they have been with Jesus," our lack of faith and trust is evident. Saul robed himself in religious flesh, wrapped himself in man-made armor, and trembled inside his tent. Saul said no to God, annulled his anointing, and relinquished his authority.

Then David arrived on the scene, a young shepherd from the hills of Bethlehem, a man so insignificant that Saul didn't even remember that David had played the harp for him just months before. Yet miraculously, David was not afraid of the strutting, self-centered Goliath! The future king in shepherd's garb stepped forward unafraid, because he had been with God.

David knew that the key to the battle was allowing the Lord God Almighty to fight for him. He knew that success lay not in Saul's much-too-big armor, but in the full armor of God.

Most Christians today do not put on the armor of God (Ephesians 6:10-18). They choose, instead, Saul's religious armor. The battles of life consume them because they fight in their own strength. Too often, they think they have won the battle, only to find that they have lost the war! They are defeated by their own words and actions. Sadly, the casualties are their children, their marriages, and their ministries.

The weapons of David's warfare were not physical, but were "mighty through God to the pulling down of strongholds." When he fought Goliath, the miracle was not so much that a stone could kill a giant, even though he had on earthly armor; it was that David knew the battle was the Lord's.

David had experienced the powerful presence of God while tending his father's sheep. He knew that the key to success was his relationship with the Lord. David was fearless in the face of his enemy, because he had been on his face in the presence of the real King of Israel.

When Goliath tossed out his challenge: "Am I a dog, that thou comest to me with staves? Come to me, and I will give thy flesh to the fowls of the air, and to the beasts of the field" (KJV), it simply bounced off David's helmet of salvation and breastplate of righteousness. David had already won the battle in his mind as he replied, "This day will the Lord deliver thee into my hand. . .that all the earth may know that there is a God in Israel."

David's greatest battle turned into his greatest blessing. He accomplished more with God in one hour than the entire nation was able to accomplish without Him. David chose to believe the words of

God over those of his brothers, Saul, and the giant. When he made the decision to believe God, David made a God-connection. Only when you believe God, and step out in faith, will you release God's power and bring about a life-change.

David's determination led him from the sheepfold to the slaughter pen, from a cave to a palace. God's favor in my own life has led me from an abusive home to a mountain of prayer, from a dark depression to the halls of presidents and prime ministers. A friend and pastor used to say, "Mike, you have favor; follow it. Some people teach prophecy; you live it."

David the hero, David the king's son-in-law, was running for his life! David had defeated Goliath, the giant Philistine. His second Goliath—Saul—was much more difficult to defeat. Do you have a Saul in your life, someone who bugs you, bothers you, and then bombs you?

The future king was now the hunted outlaw with a price on his head. Day and night for years Saul dogged David, just waiting for the moment when David would become vulnerable. The desire of Saul's heart was to plunge his spear through David.

Jealousy turns giants into jerks! Saul had a golden opportunity to demonstrate greatness when the Israelites sang, "Saul has slain his thousands, and David his ten thousands" (1 Samuel 18:7, NKJV). Saul could have taken credit for sending David into battle. He could have become bigger in the eyes of the people. Instead, he became bitter.

Your success sometimes causes people to turn on you with a jealous rage. When that happens, know that what God has told you in secret will keep you from giving up in the greatest battles of your life. Get your eyes off what you're going through and get them on what you are going to!

Wet with sweat, alone, betrayed and weary, David took refuge in the cave of Adullum. "And every one that was in distress, and every one that was in debt, and every one that was discontented, gathered themselves unto him; and he became a captain over them: and there were with him about four hundred men" (1 Samuel 22:2, KJV). There was no self-promotion for David. He was alone and cold in his cave. Things were going from bad to worse, but David refused to become a victim of "cave mentality." He was surrounded by the distressed (those under pressure or stress), by those in debt (people who could not pay their bills), and by the discontent (those bitter of soul). Did he fall into self-pity? Not David! He gathered those people around him and taught them how to become mighty warriors of valor!

Have you ever found yourself in a pit of despair—distressed, in debt, and discontented—hoping against hope that no one would come around? Step out of the darkness into the brilliant light of God's Word!

It was not God's will for David to remain in the cave; David was destined for the throne. He was in the cave, but the cave was not in him! David was content to wait on God to elevate him to the place of honor. David, the anointed shepherd-king and giant-killer, assumed the mantle of teacher and began to train his troops.

"The LORD is my light and my salvation; whom shall I fear? The

LORD is the strength of my life; of whom shall I be afraid?" (Psalm 27:1, KJV).

"But ye are a chosen generation, a royal priesthood, an holy nation, a peculiar people; that ye should show forth the praises of him who hath called you out of darkness into his marvelous light" (1 Peter 2:9, KJV).

Contentment is not the fulfillment of what you want, but the realization of how much you already have. Once you see that clearly through Christ and His Word, you will see a God bigger than your terrors.

What a scene! What incredible odds! Saul and his 3,000 special forces are pursuing David and his 400 mighty men. Saul is focused on only one thing—killing David! David, the fugitive, and his rag-tag band flee to the wilderness of Judea. They take refuge at En Gedi, which literally means "spring of the goat."

After 11 days of trekking across the Sinai, following in the footsteps of Moses, I jumped for joy at the sight of personally seeing the Spring of En Gedi. Actually, I jumped with joy into the Spring of En Gedi. It was my first bath in two weeks, and I was filthy!

Our band of 11, which included the former astronaut and later congressman Bill Nelson, and the great Christian author who is now in heaven, Jamie Buckingham, stood in awe as we gazed at the towering walls of En Gedi. It would have been the perfect place for David to hide from Saul.

DIVINE CONFRONTATION

In 1 Samuel 24:1-4, we discover a divine confrontation: "After Saul returned from pursuing the Philistines, he was told, 'David is in the Desert of En Gedi.' So Saul took three thousand chosen men from all Israel and set out to look for David and his men near the Crags of the Wild Goats. He came to the sheep pens along the way; a cave was there, and Saul went in to relieve himself. David and his men were far back in the cave. The men said, 'This is the day the LORD spoke of when he said to you, "I will give your enemy into your hands for you to deal with as you wish."' Then David crept up unnoticed and cut off a corner of Saul's robe."

Saul was delighted with the news that David had been sighted. Finally, his rival would die like a dog in the desert. But God had another plan for both David and Saul.

Needing a quiet place to refresh himself, Saul entered one of the many caves in the area, not knowing David and a handful of his men were hidden far back in the cave. Picture the scene: Saul was crouching in the privacy of the cave. He was totally vulnerable. Suddenly the kingdom was within David's grasp. A quick thrust of a spear and David would be king! His men whispered, "Do it! Kill him! He's evil; you're the chosen and anointed one. This is your moment of destiny."

David had been associate pastor of this flock for years. The path to the palace had been hard and rocky. Danger and death had been his constant companions. His congregation was full of moaners and complainers. Maybe God wanted the senior pastor out, even if it meant stabbing him in the back. Maybe David was the one to do it. After all, he was next in line to the pulpit.

Perhaps you know something about a coworker that, if revealed, would put you directly in line for that big promotion. Do you take the shortcut, or do you stick to the narrow path of divine direction?

David's vision was within his reach. One swift thrust, and he was out of the pit and into the palace. Yet he knew that "except the LORD build the house, they labor in vain that build it" (Psalm 127:1, KJV). He knew that there were no shortcuts to the throne. Even religious flesh filled with sound reasoning cannot take you to the fulfillment of your vision. David may have been at rock bottom, but he was determined to stand on the Rock and not compromise.

David's spirit was still strong. "The LORD is my light and my salvation; whom shall I fear? The LORD is the strength of my life; of whom shall I be afraid?" (Psalm 27:1, KJV).

"I waited patiently for the LORD; and he inclined unto me, and heard my cry. He brought me up also out of an horrible pit, out of the miry clay, and set my feet upon a rock, and established my goings" (Psalm 40:1-2, KJV).

The integrity of David's heart prevailed. David persuaded his men to spare Saul. "He said to his men, 'The LORD forbid that I should do such a thing to my master, the Lord's anointed, or lift my hand against him; for he is the anointed of the LORD'" (1 Samuel 24:6). Instead of murdering him, David slipped silently forward in the cave and sliced off the edge of Saul's robe.

When we take personal vengeance into our own hands, it is at great cost to our souls. Let God be God. He will vindicate. "'Vengeance is mine, I will repay,' saith the Lord" (Romans 12:19, KJV).

It has been said that the true test of character is what we do when we think no one is looking. David had passed the test. He knew that what he received in fulfillment of his desires in public would be measured by his devotion to the King in private. David embraced the promise, and God provided power during his predicament. The Holy Spirit of God moved David to create Psalms 34 and 56 at Adullum, and Psalms 31 and 54 at Ein Gedi. From the depths of despair, David wrote:

> "I will bless the Lord at all times; his praise shall continually be in my mouth," (Psalm 34:1, KJV).

> "What time I am afraid, I will trust in thee" (Psalm 56:3, KJV).

> "In thee, O Lord, do I put my trust; let me never be ashamed: deliver me in thy righteousness" (Psalm 31:1, KJV).

> "Behold, God is mine helper, the Lord is with them that uphold my soul" (Psalm 54:4, KJV).

David embraced God's Word; Saul rejected God's Word. David put God first; Saul put himself first. David fell on his face before the angel of the Lord; Saul fell on his sword, and committed suicide. David lifted his hands to present an offering (1 Samuel 30:26); Saul hid that which God told him to destroy (1 Samuel 15).

Saul's enemy wasn't David. Saul's greatest enemy was Saul, his own fleshly pride. Saul's battle was not against the Philistines; it was against God's Spirit. There was no possibility Saul could win in the Spirit what he had already lost in the flesh. Saul lost his inheritance by placing his kingship first rather than the King. Saul's choice cost him not only his inheritance; it cost him everything.

David's passion in life was to dwell in the presence of the Lord, to provide a dwelling place in his heart and in Jerusalem. This seed was planted as a young shepherd boy, watered by Samuel's anointing, and matured by Saul's pursuit and God's deliverance. David developed a heart attitude that moved God to action. David was willing to place his faith in the King and pay whatever price was necessary. Will you?

7

CONQUERING OUR SPIRITUAL ENEMY

WE WILL NEVER be able to see anything eternal without a Holy Spirit-led prayer life. The Bible says, "The heart is deceitful above all things, And desperately wicked; Who can know it?" (Jeremiah 17:9). The eyes of God search for hungry hearts willing to surrender to the person of the Holy Spirit and that thirst to be with Jesus.

SATAN'S PLANS FOR YOU

Satan's two greatest goals are (1) to convince you to live the Christian life yourself, in your own strength, and (2) to make you believe that you must be "worthy" and "righteous." With these ungodly goals achieved, disillusioned Christians continue to leave churches in droves.

Why do the unsaved resist the gospel? Because they say, "I can't live it." Why do they say this? They see Christians trying to live a Christian life in their own religious flesh and failing.

When we allow Christ to live through us, the world will run to Jesus! If Christianity were not about being with Jesus, then what would it be about? What would be the point or purpose? When the church is not about being with Jesus, it has no divine purpose or mission to influence a lost and dying world. These goals separate us from the power source that will crush Satan's head.

Christ can quench all the fiery darts of the enemy, no matter the circumstances. With self in charge, we meagerly try to please God in our own strength. But with Jesus on the throne of our lives, we experience supernatural strength.

When we fear God, we will never fear people. When we have been with Jesus, we will never surrender that intimacy to dance to another person's song. But if we spend all our energy chasing after human approval, there is no chance we can have God's. The most miserable Christian life is that of a people-pleaser. We try to live in the flesh, becoming off course and unhappy, navigating our direction by accommodating our peers, critics, and supporters. We know what to do, but instead spend our lives asking others what we ought to do. We ride a merry-go-round of repentance, regret, and recommitment.

When we are living in Jesus, we are not directed by other peoples' opinions, whether positive or negative, but filled with righteousness, peace, and joy, moved by the person of the Holy Spirit. We can be as John Knox, who caused the Queen of Scots to tremble at his prayers.

Christ is not going to take a defeated church out of this world, nor will He come back to unanswered prayers or unfulfilled prophecies. You can be assured that He is willing to kindle the fire of His life and mission in you. You can be assured that you are part of Christ's end-time strategy!

Satan's goal is to control and manipulate us, which he can only accomplish if we try to live this Christian life in our own strength. No matter how many Scriptures we quote or how sincere our intention, Satan always has the upper hand. Yet Satan has no power over us when we allow the person of Jesus Christ to live through us. We're seated in heavenly places in Christ Jesus, and it's not our flesh that is seated, it's our spirit. When we are with Jesus, Satan will wear himself out trying to frustrate us and be unsuccessful in stealing our peace and joy.

Jesus has called you into His kingdom and His glory (see 1 Thessalonians 2:12). Christ taught us to pray that God's kingdom would come, and His will would be done on earth, as it is in heaven. When Christ appeared to the men on the road to Emmaus after rising from the dead, they said to Him, "Sir, we would see Jesus."

Jesus is alive on the earth today, working through you! Can others see Him in you? Have you wrestled with God, in prayer? The patriarch Jacob, whose name was changed to Israel, wrestled with a mysterious stranger until dawn and said, ". . . I have seen God face to face, and my life is preserved" (Genesis 32:30b, KJV). Prayer is the key.

WE CANNOT SURVIVE WITHOUT PRAYER

"Go to the Killing Fields," Jesus impressed to me during prayer one day. No one had ever preached a nationwide crusade in Cambodia, where more than two million people had been slaughtered in the greatest massacre outside of the Holocaust. I took a humble pastor to the Olympic Stadium in that country and asked him, "Do you see it [the stadium] full?"

"No," he answered, "there are only 1,800 Christians in the whole nation. This stadium may hold 40-60,000. I see it empty."

"Close your eyes again and pray," I said. We prayed for more than 30 minutes. Then he saw 1,000 people in the stadium. We prayed again and as he wept, he said he saw 5,000 people. He continued crying and praying until he could see the stadium packed full. Then I said, "Now it's time to have this crusade."

God encouraged me to be bold with that communistic, totalitarian government. Through a miracle of God, the murderous Khmer Rouge government approved the crusade, and tens-of-thousands of Buddhists and Khmer Rouge murderers gathered as we proclaimed the message of Jesus Christ, crucified, resurrected, and coming again. It was the largest harvest of souls in the history of that nation.

Jesus said we cannot live by bread alone, but by every Word that proceeds out of the mouth of God. We have this power, yet we try to solve our problems ourselves! But when we've been with Jesus, we are perfumed with prayer. We become God wrestlers. The Word of God that proceeds out of our mouths and causes hell to tremble.

In the midst of the greatest revival in the history of the world, with the fullness of God's glory and power manifested, something happened one day that revolutionized the apostles. They cried, "We have to stop! We have to give ourselves to prayer!" (See Acts 6:4). Prayer is fellowship with Jesus.

Why? Didn't the apostles know that everyone wanted to hear them preach and give their testimonies? This was the occurrence that they'd waited for all these years. Why slow down a revival to stop and pray? The disciples knew the blast of God's glory coming through them was something supernatural and dynamic that was shaking hell, defeating principalities and powers. They could not jeopardize the move of God by falling prey to the appetites of their flesh. They had to keep their spirits sharp by doing as they saw their Master do and praying without ceasing.

They died to self. They waited, tarrying in prayer. It is possible to pray without surrendering to Christ; but it is impossible to surrender to Christ without praying.

Attempts to manipulate God pass as prayer today, rather than being with Jesus. Often, those who learn to "confess with their mouth" Christ's Lordship, never fully surrender to His full authority in their hearts.

We enter into God's presence through prayer! We do pray, so why don't we see His power? The great revivalist, Leonard Ravenhill, once said, "God does not answer prayer. God answers desperate prayer." Only through such prayer can we enter the intimate relationship with God for which He created us.

Only through prayer can we enter an intimate relationship with God for which He created us. Only through prayer can we truly wrestle with God.

The apostle Paul found the secret to spending time with God, and has taught us to "pray without ceasing" (1 Thessalonians 5:17) so we will "be filled with all the fullness of God" (see Ephesians 3.14-19). Paul knew this kind of prayer was essential to fulfill the purposes of God Almighty on the earth.

We say, "Lord, teach us to pray." How we need to learn to pray! To travail in desperate prayer! If we do what we have done, we will have what we have had. If we want something we have never had, we have to do something we have never done.

A life without prayer is a life without purpose and power. One day fully surrendered to the purpose of God will reap more fruit in our lives than a lifetime lived with half-hearted intentions.

THE CURSE OF PRAYERLESSNESS

Most American Christians are not praying big prayers, because they haven't *been* with Jesus. If the millions of American Christians truly cried out to God, our nation and world would be changed. Prayer is the fuel of tremendous revivals. Yet the average prayer time in the typical church service is relegated to the pastor or his associate, and lasts two to three minutes. That's the extent of the "prayer" experienced by many in the congregation for the entire week! When a prayer meeting is called, it generally only requires the smallest room. The gymnasium is packed for basketball, but the prayer closet is practically empty.

I am convinced Christians do not pray because they do not believe. We do not believe that we're living in the last days. We do not believe that we are carrying destiny, and the hope of glory. We do not believe that the Spirit of Christ within us will quicken our mortal bodies (Romans 8:11), or that we'll do greater things than Christ did because He ascended to the Father (John 14:12).

Scripture teaches, "I tell you that if two of you on earth agree about *anything* you ask for, it will be done for you by My Father in heaven. Or where two or three come together *in my name*, there am I with them" (Matthew 18:19-20, emphasis added). When we enter this realm, we are transported from "praying and hoping God will do something" to the realm of "sitting together in heavenly places in Christ Jesus" and watching Him do everything. No wonder the unsaved have run *from* church rather than *to* church. All this will change. They want help; they don't want hype.

If we understood the dynamics and power of heaven, we would pray. However, we don't understand the mission of the person of the

Holy Spirit, nor the goal of Jesus' intercession to the Father. We are tired of hearing *about* what God is going to do. We want to *see* it.

Some are praying. Thank God for a prayer movement which has sprung up, bringing forth pockets of intercessors that gather for prayer around the world. Yet many believers are still not praying.

Of those who do pray, many try to use their faith and their energies to move God to answer their obscure prayers based on culture, what they're going through, or what they feel. The Bible says we don't even know how to pray. The Spirit makes utterance for us so our prayers are based upon Jesus Christ and His mission, kingdom, and purposes.

When I was younger, we had a church tradition to "tarry" at the altar until you "prayed through." I went all night several times in those days and felt like I'd prayed only five minutes! "Praying through" means you *stay* in prayer, shut in with God in a secret place, getting sin and self out; closed in with God through the Spirit.

Samson, Israel's famous judge, relinquished to the enemy the secret of his great strength and had his eyes gouged out. While enamored with his lover Delilah, he lost sight of the danger and was caught. A slave grinding at the mill, he felt paralyzed to do anything, even though he was empowered. We give up our secret place of prayer to an enemy who distracts, destroys, and robs us of the power to live victoriously. We are blind to our own weakened condition and the power available to us, because we have been with everyone but Jesus.

When the disciples asked the Lord, "Why could we not cast [the demons] out?" His response was, "Because of your unbelief!" (Matthew 17:19-20). Prayerlessness is the bacteria growing the virus of unbelief.

The entrance into God's presence is through prayer. Jeremiah 29:13 reminds us, "You will seek me and find me when you seek me with all your heart." We seem to make time for everything that interests us, even though it means sacrifice. But to be shut in with God, and there behold His face, is a rarity. Prayerlessness is a reproach to a loving God. Prayer is our path to fellowship with God. Without it, we are without direction and blindly guided by sensual appetites. To pray in the Spirit and walk after the flesh is impossible. Desperate prayer seeks the Father's face; it is synonymous with being in Jesus' presence. Desperate prayers are prayed by those who wrestle with God.

DO IT AGAIN

When the apostle Paul wrote of two becoming one, he wasn't only speaking of marriage, but of Christ and the bride, the church (Ephesians 5:31-32). Prayer is like marriage, not because it's similar, but because God said it is a marriage in that believers are married to Christ who is the groom. Christ's power will be released through us as we consummate our marriage with Him and draw close to Him.

We must endeavor not to assume we can be joined to Christ while denying Him intimacy. We must not tell Him we'll be married to Him, but we don't want to be alone with Him. Intimacy is the mark of true marriage.

While holding an evangelistic outreach in the Congo, I heard a testimony about J.W. Tucker, a missionary in his forties, who was stoned for three hours until he died. His body was thrown into the river to be eaten by crocodiles. The tribe told the story through oral tradition (like a song or a proverb) saying, "Listen to the testimony of J. W. Tucker, whose blood was shed in the river." Years later another missionary came and said to the people, "Will you listen to the testimony of J. W. Tucker, whose blood was shed in the river?" He shared it, and a great revival broke out in that village with tremendous numbers converted.

The same thing will happen when Satan has to listen to the living testimony of Jesus Christ, whose blood was shed on the cross, and we become the torchbearers of that testimony. Such were the lives of biblical men like Moses, David, and Paul. However, God's power is not reserved for "superstars" of faith, but is available to every believer. God is looking for those who will wrestle with Him.

Remember: You can accomplish more in one hour with Jesus on the throne of your life, than in a lifetime without. Falling on our faces in prayer, armed with the understanding and revelation of the Word of God, we can each achieve the power of the cross that until now has appeared to be held in reserve for a few "choice" vessels.

"Praying through" is the channel that leads to being with Christ. Let's pray through again! It demands that we pray until our lives are totally surrendered to the Lordship of Jesus Christ. Only then can we say, as did our Lord, "Not my will, but thine be done," and literally mean it.

A SPIRITUAL BATTLE

Every time I have heard the voice of Jesus, it has been through prayer. One day Jesus softly spoke to my spirit, "You'll receive a phone call to go to the White House to pray for just one man. Give him this Scripture, 'When you pass through the waters I will be with you, and they shall not overflow you, when you walk through the fire you shall not be burnt nor shall the flames scorch you'" (see Isaiah 43:2, NKJV).

A few days later, an individual in the White House called and I asnwered. I laid hands on a man I'd never seen before and gave him the Scripture God gave me. What a shock it was within days to see the man I had prayed for, Oliver North, on the front page of the paper, being called to Congressional hearings. Several years later, he told me he stood on that blessed Scripture throughout the whole ordeal he suffered.

We tend to believe certain people or movements are anointed or blessed more than others. But the Holy Spirit is not going about anointing a person, a ministry, or a denomination. Jesus Christ is the Anointed One! The Holy Spirit doesn't affirm men or ministries; He has one goal and that is to glorify the Father.

Corrie ten Boom, the concentration camp survivor who hid Jews in her home, once told me the secret place in the Psalm 91 meant living before an audience of "One." How many people live before an audience of One? Most believers want to be affirmed by people, not by Christ.

People horribly misrepresent the Holy Spirit, saying things like, "I prayed about it and I have the witness [permission] of the Holy Spirit to divorce." If they want to destroy a person with their tongue, they say, "The Holy Spirit showed me *that* person is not right with God." Such a misuse of the Holy Spirit's name and position is despicable. Christ's ministry will not function in the lives of such people who "crucify" Him again with their words.

We have to win this spiritual battle by God's power. Compromising Christians will be devoured and devastated in the final battle for souls. The contented and casual soul will never win, because the battle is waged on our knees. True intercession is not about *me*, it's about *Him*. Intercession is focused on His heart, what moves Him, what grieves Him, what His burdens are, what His passion is, not my desires.

What-about-me Christianity breeds the bacteria of compromise. It turns preachers into prostitutes. Every week, they must come up with a new trick to keep their congregation happy! God forbid, if a minister should stand up before the congregation and act like a human being, honestly admitting that he has been discouraged, or had an argument with his wife, or has dealt with anger. If he does, many pillars of the church will nail him to the cross faster than Jesus was nailed! Flesh in such churches wants to be noticed; wants credit; wants its fair share and wants to be treated right.

An open heart precedes an open heaven. The destiny of many lies in the hands of few. Over seven billion people on earth are depending on those who will "die-to-self" and allow the life of Christ to pour through them. Jesus said, "And I, if I be lifted up from the earth, will draw all men unto Me" (John 12:32, KJV). To lift Christ up, we must disconnect from this world system.

God moves through prayer meetings. God's spotlight is looking for those who train their senses to turn away from the world and become hungry for God, listening for sounds from heaven and smelling the fragrance of prayer as all eyes are focused on Him. This is the essence of wrestling with God. The worshippers in King David's day turned their backs on the congregation, symbolizing flesh, and set their faces toward the Ark of Glory. The disciples saw the miracles of Jesus and the mighty works of Jesus, but they realized that there was only one key to His power and that was prayer. Prayer bends the ear of God.

POWER THROUGH PRAYER

Through prayer, Jesus softly spoke to me once saying He would bring together Jewish and Christian leaders of America, and that I was to announce the meeting. I did so at the next function I attended. Everyone there asked, "Where is it, and when?" I had to say I didn't know. I went home thinking I had to find a place to hold the meeting, formulate a budget, and hire a team.

Don't say a word, I felt Jesus say as I prayed. *I am greater than you think; I am closer than you think. I am more committed than you think. I am more ambitious than you think.*

"God is greater than we think" became my topic several months later when I preached at the Orange Bowl. Bobbie James, the wife of then-Governor of Alabama Fob James, came to me afterward and said she needed to fly me to Alabama because God told her He wanted to do something. Once there, the Lord told me I could share with her His vision. The State of Alabama hosted the event the Lord had spoken to me about, catered the food, brought in the Philharmonic Orchestra, and made it a truly great meeting.

I had been tempted to *help* God, working in my own strength so I could get the glory. Yet we must see ourselves in the light of Jesus Christ and realize we can do nothing in our flesh. The Old Testament priests stayed up all night before they went into the Holy of Holies the next day, because they were afraid to even have a dirty thought. Today, we have "Christian" men by the millions who are called the "priests of their homes," but who stay up all night to watch pornography online.

We must die to unbelief, lust, lying, cheating, unclean thoughts, filthy speech, dirty habits, indifference, cursing, prayerlessness, envy, backbiting, selfishness, and bitterness—anything that is unholy or grieves the Holy Spirit. Then, we can pray with great boldness:

"When thou prayest, enter into thy closet, and when thou has shut thy door, pray to thy Father which is in secret; and thy Father which seeth in secret shall reward thee openly" (Matthew 6:6, KJV).

It's time to shut the door! The Holy Spirit is passionately attempting to capture your heart and mine. Christ wants to talk with us more than we desire to talk to Him. Jesus Christ is in your prayer closet, so enter into Him, abide in Him, and let Him abide in you. Then, He will answer in powerful, unexpected ways.

When we abide in Christ, there will always be "heavenly favor." We will know if the church is abiding in Christ by the size of the waves she makes around her. The victorious church is a battleship, not a luxury cruise liner.

RUNNING FROM GOD OR TO GOD?

It's time for us to realize we are running — either from God or to God. When we've been with Jesus, we see clearly. We're not living in Old Testament times. It's not about anointed men. It's about Emmanuel, Jesus, living and dwelling in us, until we are "filled with the measure of the stature of the fullness of Christ."

The Father wants to show us Jesus and draw us to Jesus, so we can be with Jesus. Revival cannot come to our lives, our homes, our churches, or our nation until we've been with Him.

8

THE PRAYER OF JESUS
FOR OUR LIVES

THE BEST PASSAGE that describes how Jesus wanted His disciples to live in the age following His ascension, what many call the Church age—the time between His ascension and His return—is the prayer He prayed for His disciples in John 17. Take a moment to read this passage and see if any of it sounds like what you are experiencing in your life and your church gatherings:

> *These words spake Jesus, and lifted up his eyes to heaven,*
> *and said, Father, the hour is come; glorify thy Son, that thy*
> *Son also may glorify thee: As thou hast given him power*
> *over all flesh, that he should give eternal life to as many as*
> *thou hast given him. And this is life eternal, that they might*

know thee the only true God, and Jesus Christ, whom thou hast sent. I have glorified thee on the earth: I have finished the work which thou gavest me to do. And now, O Father, glorify thou me with thine own self with the glory which I had with thee before the world was.

I have manifested thy name unto the men which thou gavest me out of the world: thine they were, and thou gavest them me; and they have kept thy word. Now they have known that all things whatsoever thou hast given me are of thee. For I have given unto them the words which thou gavest me; and they have received them, and have known surely that I came out from thee, and they have believed that thou didst send me. I pray for them: I pray not for the world, but for them which thou hast given me; for they are thine. And all mine are thine, and thine are mine; and I am glorified in them.

And now I am no more in the world, but these are in the world, and I come to thee. Holy Father, keep through thine own name those whom thou hast given me, that they may be one, as we are. While I was with them in the world, I kept them in thy name: those that thou gavest me I have kept, and none of them is lost, but the son of perdition; that the scripture might be fulfilled. And now come I to thee; and these things I speak in the world, that they might have my joy fulfilled in themselves. I have given them thy word;

and the world hath hated them, because they are not of the world, even as I am not of the world. I pray not that thou shouldest take them out of the world, but that thou shouldest keep them from the evil. They are not of the world, even as I am not of the world.

Sanctify them through thy truth: thy word is truth. As thou hast sent me into the world, even so have I also sent them into the world. And for their sakes I sanctify myself, that they also might be sanctified through the truth.

Neither pray I for these alone, but for them also which shall believe on me through their word; That they all may be one; as thou, Father, art in me, and I in thee, that they also may be one in us: that the world may believe that thou hast sent me. And the glory which thou gavest me I have given them; that they may be one, even as we are one: I in them, and thou in me, that they may be made perfect in one; and that the world may know that thou hast sent me, and hast loved them, as thou hast loved me.

Father, I will that they also, whom thou hast given me, be with me where I am; that they may behold my glory, which thou hast given me: for thou lovedst me before the foundation of the world. O righteous Father, the world hath not known thee: but I have known thee, and these have known that thou hast sent me. And I have declared unto them thy name, and will declare it: that the love wherewith *thou hast loved me may be in them, and I in them* (John 17:1-26).

In studying this passage I have found nine particular prayers of Jesus that have not fully come to pass in the lives of believers today—nine petitions that appear to remain unanswered.

In this passage, Jesus is praying for His disciples, but in verse 20 He says, "Neither pray I for these alone, but for them also which shall believe on me through their word." Believers in all the centuries following are included in this prayer, because we are those who have believed on Christ through the Word and testimony of the disciples. When Jesus prayed for his disciples in John 17, He was also praying for us.

How is it that Jesus' own prayers might yet be unfulfilled? Before we discuss that, let's look at what they were:

1) We would know the only true God (see John 17:3),

2) We would be one as He and His Father are one (see John 17:21),

3) We would have His joy (see John 17:13),

4) We would be kept from evil (see John 17:15),

5) We would be sanctified through the truth (see John 17:19),

6) We would behold His glory (see John 17:24),

7) We would be made perfect (see John 17:23),

8) The world would know that we have been with Jesus (see John 17:22-23, 25, and Acts 4:13), and

9) The love of God would be released to the world through us (see John 17:26).

These prayers have been partially answered from time to time and in the lives of individuals, but Jesus was praying for His body as a whole, to the church. Can we honestly say that these prayers have been wholly answered when you look at so-called Christians today? Do we know God? Have we become one with Him? Have we been perfected? Do His joy, love, and glory pour forth in our lives? You must surely admit that the church on earth today is a far cry from the "glorious church, not having spot, or wrinkle, or any such thing" (Ephesians 5:27) for which He plans to return. Could it be that we, His body on earth, have failed to understand and fulfill His will for our lives?

Perhaps the best example of this is that it is God's will for all to be saved (1 Timothy 2:3-4), but are all then automatically saved? No! We must make our own choice to accept Jesus as Lord and Savior. It is with our mouth that we must confess Jesus as Lord and with our heart that we believe God raised Him from the dead in order to be saved (see Romans 10:9-10). Your father can't do that for you and your mother can't do that for you. We have the choice of whether or not to connect with what God has already provided. It is just as if I went to the store and bought a present for my wife, and took it home and gave it to her. Though it is bought and paid for and truly belongs to her, she will never be able to use it until she decides to unwrap the box and accept the gift!

So it is with God's will for our lives. Jesus paid the price for our salvation through His death on the cross. Unless you and I are willing to receive His gift, it is forever lost to us. No matter how much our hearts cry out to have His will accomplished in our lives, we must first receive His gift of salvation according to His Word.

When I first realized all of this, I suddenly began to better understand the dissatisfaction I had expressed in my professor's office as a college student. My heart was crying out for God's will in my life; my spirit was expressing dissatisfaction in conforming to the world's way of living and thinking about how one should become a believer. My heart told me there had to be something more.

Then, when I recognized that not all Christ's prayers had been completely answered and that if I would make myself available to Him I could be instrumental in their being fulfilled, I received a sense of destiny that gave my life purpose and meaning. Suddenly divine truth penetrated the core of my being and my life mattered! The purpose for my life—and for the life of every Christian on this earth—is to stand in agreement with our Lord and Savior for his prayers to be fully answered, just as I stood in agreement with His will for me to be saved.

It was as if a giant vacuum had begun to remove the dross from my life. The clouds of confusion vanished from my mind, and the burdensome oughts and shoulds fell off my shoulders. All I had to do was pray in agreement with Christ, walk in agreement with His Spirit, and then see His prayers answered in the world around me! When believers come together in what we traditionally call church with a desire to see His prayers answered, it is at that point where heaven and earth meet, where the mind of Christ can be revealed, and His power made manifest.

This is the answer to every person's identity, destiny, inferiority, or insecurity. We have no purpose, we have no meaning, and our destiny is unsecured because Christ's prayers are not yet completely answered. All we have to do is pay attention to His prayers and be obedient to His direction regarding how to fulfill them.

JESUS WANTS YOU

The disciples did have an advantage: They had been with Jesus and seen His Father's will work through Him every day for three years. When He left them, and they received the Holy Spirit on the Day of Pentecost, they had a living example of how to operate in what they had received. Yet, in truth, the greatest among them had never experienced any of that!

The apostle Paul had never followed Jesus around the towns and villages of Israel watching Him heal the sick, cast out demons, and raise the dead. Perhaps that is why he left us the most explicit instructions for living the Christian life. He wrote more epistles that became part of the New Testament than any other. We certainly don't have the advantage that the disciples had of walking with Jesus, but we do have the same resources, and more, than Paul had. We have the complete Bible, Old and New Testaments, to guide us to live according to His truth.

We need to read what these men of God wrote about Jesus and simply believe it, rejecting whatever others may have told us we are to expect. God will not contradict His Word, but He will often confirm. It is time for us to pay attention to the prayers Jesus prayed for us.

GOD, USE ME

My prayer in Jerusalem on February 17, 1993 was, "God, I'm hungry. I want to know you. Will you use me?" The funny thing is this was not at the beginning of my Christian walk, nor even the beginning of my ministry. I was already established as a minister. I had been to the White House to serve on advisory boards comprised of ministers. I had been a guest on national television and radio talk shows. I was speaking regularly at churches and events, and met often with world leaders. *My* ministry was doing fine. The problem was that I no longer wanted to do *my* ministry; I wanted to do *Jesus'* ministry.

I had come to realize that I knew a lot about Jesus and could talk about Him for hours, but I didn't really know Him. Here I was trying to serve Jesus with all of *my* mind and *my* strength, and I was failing because I didn't really even know Him! I was desperate to change that—and as He always does, God began to answer my desperate prayers.

DO WE KNOW JESUS, OR ONLY KNOW ABOUT HIM?

In John 17:3, Jesus prayed that we "might know the only true God, and Jesus Christ, whom thou hast sent." Yet most Christians today seem content to go through life with what they or someone else thinks about God rather than truly knowing Him for themselves. The truth of the matter is, most of us are content to go to church and hear about God, His Son, and His Holy Spirit, but if He were ever to ask us to meet with Him personally, we would be too terrified to comply!

When Israel had been led forth from Egypt by Moses, had been saved by passing through the Red Sea, and had seen God's miraculous provision of manna, quail, and water from a rock in the desert, you would think that they knew God well—but in fact they still refused to draw near to Him. Even though they had seen Moses climb the mountain and return unharmed, his face glowing with the glory of the Lord, they chose to have someone else stand between them and God because they feared knowing God personally. Moses recorded it this way:

> And it came to pass, when ye heard the voice out of the
> midst of the darkness, (for the mountain did burn with
> fire,) that ye came near unto me, even all the heads of

your tribes, and your elders; And ye said, Behold, the LORD our God hath shewed us his glory and his greatness, and we have heard his voice out of the midst of the fire: we have seen this day that God doth talk with man, and he liveth.

Now therefore why should we die? for this great fire will consume us: if we hear the voice of the LORD our God any more, then we shall die. For who is there of all flesh, that hath heard the voice of the living God speaking out of the midst of the fire, as we have, and lived? Go thou near, and hear all that the LORD our God shall say: and speak thou unto us all that the LORD our God shall speak unto thee; and we will hear it, and do it (Deuteronomy 5:23-27, KJV).

In other words, though they knew of God's greatness, His miracle-working power to deliver, and had heard Him speak from the cloud that had descended upon the mountaintop, they did not want to get too close to Him because of fear. They said, "Go thou near." In other words, "Moses, you go and talk to God. You find out His plans. Then come and tell us. We will do whatever He wants, but we just don't want to have to get that close to Him."

Are we really any different today? We flock to churches to do what? Hear from God? Heavens, no! We flock to church to hear others tell us what they have learned about God. But to take time to get on our knees and seek God for ourselves? Get our instructions from God first hand through His Word? Draw near and get to know God and his nature for ourselves? Can you and I really cast aside our fear and do that?

Don't misunderstand, learning from pastors and teachers in the church is important, but are you adding their teachings to the knowledge of God you have attained through time spent with Him? Or, are they your sole source for learning about God? One of our biggest hindrances to knowing God is that we don't really believe we *can* know Him. Think about it. The Bible is filled with promises by God to know Him if we are just willing to draw near, but do you know God even as well as some of your acquaintances? Is He the first one you go to for advice, to share your financial needs, or to spend free time? How well do we—any of us—really know God?

JESUS CAME TO A PEOPLE WHO NO LONGER KNEW GOD

When Jesus began His ministry, He was constantly confronted by religious leaders to whom the same Old Testament offers to know God had been made. But they chose rather to live within the confines of the Law instead of drawing near to Him through His Son, Jesus Christ. They spent more time attempting to make His Word harsh and unforgiving than in studying the Scriptures. They spent no time with God individually or corporately, and much time in perfecting the art of religion for show.

They sat and listened to men debate their own opinions about God until they were so far removed from His heart that they were ready to condemn God in the person of Jesus as a heretic and a blasphemer when He offered truth to them! Think about it! Throughout history, how many have been condemned by the church itself as heretics when in fact they were diligently trying to lead people back to true worship, true religion, and a true relationship with God? When Jesus returns for His bride, the church, will He find that His betrothed doesn't know Him?

God forbid! Instead the Scriptures say:

> Christ also loved the church, and gave himself for it; That he might sanctify and cleanse it with the washing of water by the word, That he might present it to himself a glorious church, not having spot, or wrinkle, or any such thing; but that it should be holy and without blemish (Ephesians 5:24-27).

Could this possibly be a church that knows Him as little as we do today?

CAN WE BE FRIENDS WITH GOD?

God has always revealed Himself to those who truly desire to know Him—and such were called the friends of God. The Bible says of Abraham:

Abraham believed God, and it was imputed unto him for righteousness: and he was called the Friend of God (James 2:23 KJV).

Art not thou our God, who didst drive out the inhabitants of this land before thy people Israel, and gavest it to the seed of Abraham thy friend forever? (2 Chronicles 20:7, KJV).

Why was he called God's friend? Abraham was a man who communicated with God directly, making a covenant with him through the blood sacrifice of animals (Genesis 15:7-17) and circumcision (Genesis 17:1-14), pleading for the people of Sodom and Gomorrah (Genesis 18:22-33), and obedient even to the death of his own son (Genesis 22:1-18). He was a man who knew God through direct contact with Him and became the father of two covenants, both the Old Covenant to the Jews and the New Covenant, because his willingness to sacrifice his own son for God was the precursor of God's willingness to sacrifice his own Son for humanity. Abraham knew God personally by spending time with Him continually.

Look what the Bible says of Jacob, the man who wrestled with God until he received His blessing:

And he [God] said, Thy name shall be called no more Jacob, but Israel: for as a prince hast thou power with God and with men, and hast prevailed. . . . And Jacob called the name of the place Peniel: for I have seen God face to face, and my life is preserved (Genesis 32:28, 30).

It was through coming face-to-face with God that Jacob came to know Him and have power with God and men.

Look at what the Bible says about Moses:

And the LORD spake unto Moses face to face, as a man speaketh unto his friend (Exodus 33:11, KJV).

Why was this? Look at the desires of Moses' heart as expressed in this prayer that appears just a few verses later:

I pray thee, if I have found grace in thy sight, show me now thy way, that I may know thee, that I may find grace in thy sight: and consider that this nation is thy people. . . . If thy presence go not with me, carry us not up hence. For wherein shall it be known here that I and thy people have found grace in thy sight? is it not in that thou goest with us? so shall we be separated, I and thy people, from all the people that are upon the face of the earth. . . . I beseech thee, show me thy glory (Exodus 33:13, 15-16, 18, KJV).

Moses knew God because he had experienced Him personally. Many think that knowing God is the privilege of a chosen few—those selected from each generation—Abraham, Moses, David, Paul. These were men who waited on God, spent tremendous time alone in prayer with Him, men whose hearts desired nothing else but to know God. And it has always been people like these men with such uncompromisingly desperate hearts to whom God has revealed Himself. God chooses, yet He also uses those devoted to Him.

GETTING TO KNOW HIM

If you really desire to know Jesus, it is not much different than getting acquainted with another person. If one wanted to get to know a famous person, for example, the first step would be to read their biography or research them on the Internet. The biography of Jesus is widely available in the Gospels. The accounts of those who walked with Jesus are included, as are those of the apostle Paul in Acts, the various epistles, and letters from James, John, Peter, and Jude. As in getting to know another person, the best way to become familiar with Jesus is to spend time talking with Him, and listening carefully to what He has to say through His Word. In Matthew 11:28-29 (KJV) Jesus said to His disciples:

> Come unto me, all ye that labour and are heavy laden,
> and I will give you rest. Take my yoke upon you, and
> learn of me; for I am meek and lowly in heart: and ye
> shall find rest unto your souls.

This is the opportunity we have through prayer; we can talk with

Him in a quiet place, and get to know His heart by listening with spiritual ears.

However, if we come to that meeting with preconceived notions and do all the talking ourselves, we know no more about that person when we leave than when we arrived. If we are truly going to know Him, then we must set aside any preconceived notions and come to Him ready and willing to learn. We can learn to recognize and discern His voice more clearly and then compare what we hear during times spent in His Word; He will never contradict Himself. As He said in John 10:

> *He who enters by the door is a shepherd of the sheep. To him the doorkeeper opens, and the sheep hear his voice, and he calls his own sheep by name and leads them out. When he puts forth all his own, he goes ahead of them, and the sheep follow him because they know his voice. . . ."I am the good shepherd"* (John 10:2-4, 11 NASB).

Notice that the sheep have learned the voice of the shepherd because they have lived closely with him for some time. The shepherd does not just drop by once a week to spend an hour or so with the sheep; the animals make their way by following the shepherd. They go where he leads and nowhere else. They don't choose a field and then try to convince the shepherd to come there; they only eat from the fields and drink from the streams where he leads them:

The LORD is my shepherd; I shall not want. He maketh me to lie down in green pastures: he leadeth me beside the still waters. He restoreth my soul: he leadeth me in the paths of righteousness for his name's sake (Psalm 23:1-3, KJV).

It is time to really get to know God, not to just know about Him. Sincere believers can impede what God is trying to do on the earth today because they are content to be Christians outwardly, all the while continuing to follow their own inward desires (1 Corinthians 3:1-3). The same thing that happened to the religious people in the time of Jesus is happening today: We follow God through a prescribed list of do's and don'ts as opposed to having a living relationship with the Holy God.

There was a time I would have scoffed at the thought that I was living by a list of rules rather than following Christ personally. I discovered that my actions were more dictated by trying to impress others with my so-called Christianity than by having the same priorities as God.

In the 1980s, I was intoxicated with power and had no idea how deceived I was in my fleshly pursuits. During the early days of the Reagan era, I was on the VIP list, and was invited time and again to the White House. Oh my, I had arrived! One day I would have lunch with the President of the United States or a member of his Cabinet, in the company of other religious leaders. Another time, I might be in a special briefing with Secretary of State Robert McFarland, challenging him concerning the Word of God.

I was also once asked to briefly address the Republican National Convention when it met in Dallas, Texas, for a special session. Following that, I was invited to a reception with the President's Cabinet and some of the most powerful people in the world. But one day as I was having lunch in the White House with the President and members of his Cabinet, the stench of my flesh wafted up and hit me in the face. I was sitting next to Charles Colson, former Special Counsel to President Richard Nixon. He had been imprisoned following the Watergate Scandal.

"Chuck," I said, "have you been back since Watergate?"

"No," he said, "this is my first time."

"You must be happy about these strategies under discussion, especially since you had a lot to do with them."

"No, it's the last thing on my mind," he said. "I just felt the Lord wanted me to come, but what I'm really excited about is going to visit death row inmates tonight to share the gospel."

Looking at Chuck, I saw such brokenness and humility. He was anticipating his appointment with Jesus that night at the death house, not the White House. Yet many of us in that room were pushing and shoving, scheming and conniving to have our pictures taken with the President, saying a few words or slipping a note to him. Christ must surely have been weeping. The only "Who's Who" list He cares about is whose name is written in the Lamb's Book of Life.

I was so polluted and yet I was strutting like a rooster—arrogant, proud, hot-tempered, and even offended when my wife did not treat me like royalty. Didn't she realize that I'm a man of God and a very, very important one at that? What a stench in the nostrils of God!

God does not need us, but we desperately need Him. We are called to faithfully serve His will, not our own.

9

OUR PRAYER TO JESUS: THE LORD'S PRAYER

IN THE ENTIRE BIBLE, Jesus only taught His disciples one prayer, which we call the Lord's Prayer today. Though many of us recite it from memory in services or on special occasions, how often do we really think about it or expect this prayer to be answered? Look again and think about praying this prayer as if you were binding yourself with its words and with God to see these requests accomplished on the earth:

Our Father which art in heaven, Hallowed be thy name.

Thy kingdom come. Thy will be done in earth, as it is in heaven.

Give us this day our daily bread.

And forgive us our debts, as we forgive our debtors.

And lead us not into temptation, but deliver us from evil: For thine is the kingdom, and the power, and the glory, for ever. Amen (Matthew 6:9-13, KJV).

This simple and profound prayer says:

1) I worship and praise You,

2) I want Your kingdom to be realized on earth just as it is in heaven,

3) I will trust in Your provision,

4) I will forgive others as You have forgiven me,

5) Through Your strength, I will resist temptation and avoid evil,

6) Because You are the owner of the kingdom, power, and glory that will last forever,

7) Amen (Which means "so let it be").

To me, everything that is wrapped up in being a Christian is in this prayer and the main purpose of being a Christians is right there at the beginning: "Thy kingdom come. They will be done on earth, as it is in heaven." The true purpose of the church—the body of Christ on the earth—is simply to see His will done here as it is in heaven.

THE KINGDOM OF HEAVEN

Look for a moment at the things to which Jesus compared the kingdom of heaven:

1) A grain of mustard seed—it may start as the smallest of all things, but when it is planted and grows, it becomes a place of shelter, lodging, and protection (see Matthew 13:31-32).

2) Yeast—though it is only added to a small part of something, it will soon permeate and change everything it comes into contact with (see Matthew 13:33).

3) A hidden treasure and a pearl of great price—for the joy of having this one thing, a person would be willing to sell everything they own to possess it (see Matthew 13:44-45), and those who trust in their wealth and possessions rather than in God will have a hard time entering into it (see Mark 10:23-26.).

4) A net—which when it is cast in the sea will return full to the boat with every kind of fish (see Matthew 13:47-50).

5) A man hiring workers for his vineyard and a king inviting guests to his son's wedding—those who come to it will receive its reward whether they come early or late, and though many are invited, only those who answer that call will enjoy its benefits: "For many are called, but few are chosen" (See Matthew 20:1-16;).

Jesus admonished us to pray that His will be done on earth as in heaven. This is what the church was meant to do—usher in His kingdom. How can we possibly fulfill this assignment if we do not truly know Him and are one with Him?

Jesus gave a simple illustration to His disciples. I think many of us tend to miss a nuance of this teaching that would help to clarify His instructions. Please carefully read the following passage:

> *At the same time came the disciples unto Jesus, saying, Who is the greatest in the kingdom of heaven?*
>
> *And Jesus called a little child unto him, and set him in the midst of them, And said, Verily I say unto you, Except ye be converted, and become as little children, ye shall not enter into the kingdom of heaven. Whosoever therefore shall humble himself as this little child, the same is greatest in the kingdom of heaven.* (Matthew 18:1-4, KJV).

Most of us have heard this story before, and have come away with the message that we should be like little children before God if we want to enter His kingdom. We have centered on the point that we should have the attributes of children—innocence, trustfulness, simplicity—the central meaning of this passage. And this certainly is an important part of it, but it is not the answer to the disciples' question. Look at the passage again, and you will see Jesus' response is two-fold: 1) Except that you become as a little child, you shall not enter the kingdom of heaven; and 2) Whoever shall humble himself as a little child shall become the greatest in the kingdom of heaven.

Jesus is being very specific here in this second point: It is not the general principle of childlikeness that will usher us into God's kingdom on earth, but there is something special about this one child that will teach us great things about living in God's kingdom. Was it the identity of the child? Was he a saint who would do great things in life? Was Jesus showing the disciples someone they should look to for guidance after He was gone?

The passage offers no suggestion of this. In fact, the key to Jesus' teaching is plainly in what He said: "Whosoever therefore shall humble himself as this little child . . ." The point was not in who the child was, but in what the child did. How did he humble himself? He simply did what Jesus asked without question or hesitation.

Picture the scene again: The disciples asked Jesus a question, and in response Jesus turned around and saw a little boy walking by, perhaps carrying water for his parents or on some other task. He may simply have been running down the street playing with some friends. Jesus said, "Child," catching the boy's attention, "come here." The boy stopped what he was doing, however important his errand or however much he may have been enjoying his play, and walked obediently to Jesus.

He didn't say, "Sure, Jesus, just as soon as I finish what I am doing." Nor did he say, "Aw, come on, can't I finish my game first?"

No, he went immediately, without saying a word. Then Jesus took the boy lovingly by the shoulders and turned him to face the disciples and said, "Whosoever shall humble himself as this little child, the same is greatest in the kingdom of heaven."

This is what I have experienced again and again in my life, though more often by accident than intent. At times when I was completely dependent upon God, knowing I could do nothing in my own strength, stripped of all self-confidence, my desperate prayer would be, "God if You don't do it, it can't be done." Then I simply did what God told me to do in response. I often had no idea that the desperate cry of my heart was the fertile soil in which the glory of God would be manifested. Now I see clearly that those times when Jesus moved the most powerfully were when I learned to lean heavily upon Him. He has moved most powerfully when "I" moved out of the way. Jesus would show up and softly speak, and when I obeyed, I would see His will done on earth as if we were actually standing before His throne in heaven. This is receiving the kingdom of God like a child.

Suffer the little children to come unto me, and forbid them not: for of such is the kingdom of God. Verily I say unto you, Whosoever shall not receive the kingdom of God as a little child, he shall not enter therein (Mark 10:14-15, KJV).

It is through those that have spent time with Jesus—and obey His voice—that His kingdom becomes real on the earth.

MANY PARTS; ONE PURPOSE

Please don't misunderstand what I am about to say here: I am not calling for some ecumenical movement among all those who call themselves Christians to join together into one universal, corporate church organization. I only want to know: Do you know Jesus? Have you been with Him? Are you taking part in His plans to bring to fruition His kingdom on the earth? Are you obeying His unique plan for your life? Are you one with Him?

If each of us would just be one with Jesus, then we would have no problem working together on the earth to usher in His kingdom, no matter what we want to call ourselves or what our function is in His plan. This is why His church is compared to a body with many parts with all having different functions, but working together to build itself up in unity of purpose and the love of God. Look at how Paul described it in Ephesians:

Therefore it says,

"WHEN HE ASCENDED ON HIGH,

HE LED CAPTIVE A HOST OF CAPTIVES,

AND HE GAVE GIFTS TO MEN."

. . . for the equipping of the saints for the work of service, to the building up of the body of Christ; until we all attain to the unity of the faith, and of the knowledge of the Son of God, to a mature man, to the measure of the stature which belongs to the fullness of Christ.

As a result, we are no longer to be children, tossed here and there by waves and carried about by every wind of doctrine, by the trickery of men, by craftiness in deceitful scheming; but speaking the truth in love, we are to grow up in all aspects into Him who is the head, even Christ, from whom the whole body, being fitted and held together by what every joint supplies, according to the proper working of each individual part, causes the growth of the body for the building up of itself in love (Ephesians 4:8, 13-16 NASB).

David wrote of it in this way:

Behold, how good and how pleasant it is for brethren to dwell together in unity! It is like the precious ointment upon the head, that ran down upon the beard, even Aaron's beard: that went down to the skirts of his garments; As the dew of Hermon, and as the dew that descended upon the mountains of Zion: for there the LORD commanded the blessing, even life for evermore (Psalm 133).

The word "together" here emphasizes a plurality in unity. David is describing the place where brothers and sisters work together in this kind of unity. It is the place of God's anointing! It is a place where we are refreshed and strengthened by God's Spirit as the dew nourishes the grass! It is the place where God commands blessing! And it is the place where life flows freely.

Only when self is subjugated to Christ will we be one with God—and each other—to have this kind of unity. We will never be one by trying to agree with each other and putting aside differences of belief for the sake of unity alone. We are to be one as Jesus and His Father are one. Only when Jesus is on the throne in each of our lives can we be in tune with His purpose and be one body on earth able to work corporately to bring true and lasting revival. Only when self is subjugated to Jesus will His greater works flourish as the body of Christ grows into His fullness and carries forth His kingdom on the earth. This is what atonement—"at-one-ment"—is all about: We must be one with Jesus.

LIVING WITH JESUS' JOY

The days must have been dark for all the Israelites. The city around them lay in ruins. Even as they struggled to rebuild and repair it, they carried with them the constant fear that they would be attacked again. They worked with mortar, trowel, or a stone in one hand, and a spear or sword for defense in the other. Stone by stone, they rebuilt the wall, watching the hills around them for any sign of attack. Only occasionally did they allow their watchfulness to drift to thoughts of the day when the city walls would be fully repaired and they could leave this labor for the work of rebuilding the temple. Their hope was in a God of whom they knew very little; yet, they longed for His presence to once again dwell in their midst.

When the walls were finally completed, the people gathered on the first day of the seventh month, the beginning of the Feast of Trumpets, and the priest mounted a platform to address the crowds. There, he opened the Book. At this, the people stood. From early morning until midday he read the law that had been given through Moses. In response to hearing the Word of their Lord that had been so far removed from them during their time of exile, the people shouted praises and called out "Amen! Amen! So be it! So be it!" They wept under the conviction that they had so freely and unknowingly violated God's laws without even realizing it. Many fell to their faces on the ground and cried out for forgiveness, their tears mixing with the dust.

At the sight of their lamentations, their leader Nehemiah rose before them and called out:

"Don't weep on such a day as this! For today is a sacred day before the LORD your God. . . .

> "Go and celebrate with a feast of choice foods and sweet drinks, and share gifts of food with people who have nothing prepared. This is a sacred day before our Lord. Don't be dejected and sad, for the joy of the LORD is your strength!" (Nehemiah 8:9-10, NLT).

The Scriptures also record the people's response to this:

So the people went away to eat and drink at a festive meal, to share gifts of food, and to celebrate with great joy because they had heard God's words and understood them (Nehemiah 8: 12 NLT).

The next day the people rose up and began to do what they had heard and understood from God's Word. They desired that all in the region who didn't grasp it would know and understand His Law so they could each walk in it and keep His ways. (See Nehemiah 7:73-8:18).

I am sure that many of you have heard Nehemiah 8:10: "The joy of the Lord is your strength." But how many are familiar with the story behind it? In the midst of a people defeated, fearful, and trying to rebuild their nation and faith came revival and a return to the Word of God.

This renewal brought guilt and tears of conviction from those who knew they had been ignorant to the truth of God's Word. All their lives, the people had called upon and reverenced His name, but knew little of His laws. It was into this atmosphere that Nehemiah spoke these often-repeated words.

Are Christians worldwide who are trying to rebuild our faith and our defenses in the face of terrorism, recession, corporate scandals, pandemics, a volatile stock market, and other chaotic events that much different than those working to rebuild Jerusalem during the days of Nehemiah? My word to you is the same as Nehemiah's was to the people of God in his time: "Stop your crying and rejoice! It is time to see His Word accomplished! For the joy of the Lord Jesus is your strength!"

THE JOY OF YOUR LORD

In John 17, the third prayer Jesus prayed for his followers was "that they might have my joy fulfilled in themselves" (John 17:13). Imagine that, living in the same joy in which Jesus lived while on the earth! That is an amazing prayer and a remarkable challenge to the body of Christ. Would anyone looking at the church today really call its members joyful? Would they even call them a happy people? The fact is that our churches are filled with discouraged, unhappy people looking for fulfillment. We are God's frozen chosen—His own pickled people—sitting in our pews and daring our ministers to make us smile. Is this the body that has been called to live in Jesus' joy?

It is, but it is not the body fulfilling its calling to live in His joy. Where have we missed the target? How can the church once again become "a chosen generation, a royal priesthood, an holy nation, a peculiar people; that ye should shew forth the praises of him who hath called you out of darkness into his marvelous light" (1 Peter 2:9, KJV).

Before we can answer that we must first understand exactly what Jesus' joy was. A quick word search of the Scriptures will show some interesting aspects of joy. In the Old Testament, we see joy expressed by the people of Israel when they had been victorious in battle, when David brought the Ark of the Covenant back to Jerusalem, when Solomon was crowned king to succeed his father, and when the temple was finally rebuilt and rededicated in the time of Ezra and Nehemiah. When Israel was delivered from Babylonian captivity, the Psalmist expressed it this way:

> When the LORD turned again the captivity of Zion, we were like them that dream. Then was our mouth filled with laughter, and our tongue with singing: then said they among the heathen, The LORD hath done great things for them. The LORD hath done great things for us; wheref we are glad.
>
> Turn again our captivity, O LORD, as the streams in the south. They that sow in tears shall reap in joy. He that goeth forth and weepeth, bearing precious seed, shall doubtless come again with rejoicing, bringing his sheaves with him (Psalm 126:1-6).

The book of Proverbs also tells us, "The desire accomplished is sweet to the soul" (Proverbs 13:19).

In the New Testament, Jesus gives an example of what joy is when he is preparing his disciples for His crucifixion and resurrection:

> Verily, verily, I say unto you, That ye shall weep and lament, but the world shall rejoice: and ye shall be

sorrowful, but your sorrow shall be turned into joy. A woman when she is in travail hath sorrow, because her hour is come: but as soon as she is delivered of the child, she remembereth no more the anguish, for joy that a man is born into the world. And ye now therefore have sorrow: but I will see you again, and your heart shall rejoice, and your joy no man taketh from you (John 16:20-22, KJV).

John the Baptist gave this example:

They came to John and said to him, "Rabbi, that man who was with you on the other side of the Jordan—the one you testified about—well, he is baptizing, and everyone is going to him."

To this John replied, "A man can receive only what is given him from heaven. You yourselves can testify that I said, 'I am not the Christ but am sent ahead of him.' The bride belongs to the bridegroom. The friend who attends the bridegroom waits and listens for him, and is full of joy when he hears the bridegroom's voice. That joy is mine, and it is now complete. He must become greater; I must become less" (John 3:26-30).

Elsewhere in the Gospels, we see joy expressed at the birth and resurrection of Jesus and with the return of the 70 after Jesus had sent them out to, "Heal the sick, cleanse the lepers, raise the dead, cast out devils" (Matthew 10:8). In the book of Acts, we also see joy when many were healed in Samaria, when Peter was delivered from prison by the angel in answer to the prayers of the early believers, and at various times during the missionary trips of Paul when believers heard that others had received the Word of God and accepted Jesus.

If you look closely at these examples you will discover some interesting things about joy:

1) Joy comes after victory—and victory does not come without a battle or a struggle (as after a war or the birth of a child).

2) People turn from tears to joy—joy often comes after a period of sorrow or loss (as at the time of exile coming to an end).

3) Joy comes when something long hoped for is finally manifested (as after the fulfillment of prophecy—such as the coming of the Messiah).

4) Joy always seems to come in connection with the will of God being done (as at the receiving of the Word of God by others after persecutions or when Israel was delivered from her seventy years of exile).

Joy, which is internal and constant, can be contrasted with happiness which is dependent on outward circumstances. Contentment is a state in which we choose to be satisfied for those things we already possess. Joy comes when something hoped for has been realized. The Psalmist wrote in Psalm 30:5 (KJV): "weeping may endure for a night, but joy cometh in the morning" Our joy should be based on a constant—our relationship with God—and not on feelings.

Look at another example Jesus gave in the parable of the talents:

> And so he that had received five talents came and brought other five talents, saying, Lord, thou deliveredst unto me five talents: behold, I have gained beside them five talents more. His lord said unto him, Well done, thou good and faithful servant: thou hast been faithful over a few things, I will make thee ruler over many things: enter thou into the joy of thy lord. He also that had received two talents came and said, Lord, thou deliveredst unto me two talents: behold, I have gained two other talents beside them. His lord said unto him, Well done, good and faithful servant; thou hast been faithful over a few things, I will make thee ruler over many things: enter thou into the joy of thy lord (Matthew 25:20-23, KJV).

In this parable, Jesus likens the kingdom of God to a man who has gone away and left tasks for his servants. Those who entered into "the joy of their Lord" were those who used what He gave them to increase His kingdom and those who were reproved were those that did nothing with what they were given. Entering into His Joy thus comes from fulfilling His tasks on the earth with what He has given us!

This was Jesus' joy—fulfilling the will of His Father. The Bible tells us in the book of Hebrews, "Jesus . . . who for the joy that was set before him endured the cross, despising the shame" (Hebrews 12:2). When do we see Jesus the most joyful and satisfied in the gospels?

After he had spoken to the woman at the well in Samaria (John 4):

> I have meat to eat that ye know not of. . . . My meat is to do the will of him that sent me, and to finish his work (John 4:32, 34, KJV).

When others showed unprecedented faith (the Roman Centurion and the Syrophoenician woman):

> When Jesus heard it, he marveled, and said to them that followed, Verily I say unto you, I have not found so great faith, no, not in Israel (Matthew 8:10, KJV).

When the seventy returned to Him, having walked in His miraculous power:

> And the seventy returned again with joy, saying, Lord,

even the devils are subject unto us through thy name. . . .
In that hour Jesus rejoiced in spirit (Luke 10:17, 21, KJV).

All these were cases where the will of God was manifested on the earth. Jesus' joy was that His Father's will be done on earth as it is in heaven.

JOY IS WON

What does the joy of Jesus include? We find Jesus:

1) Knew God's will,

2) Aligned Himself with that will, and

3) Did what God had instructed Him to do through the Holy Spirit to make that will a reality.

Joy comes from knowing the will of God, aligning ourselves with it through prayer and agreement with His Word, and acting according to the leadership of His Holy Spirit. Until we truly know God, realize a sense of His purpose and mission for our lives, plug into it, and begin to walk in it, we will not know joy the same way Jesus did. While we may feel happy, be blessed and have contentment, we will never experience His true joy except in the fulfillment of God's purposes for our lives or in the lives of those around us. Real joy is grounded in the fulfillment of the will of God. It comes from knowing and fulfilling the Word and will of God!

CAN JOY BE TAKEN AWAY?

Many of us have probably experienced at least a bit of His joy when we saw a friend saved or when we experienced the will of God in ourselves or someone we know. But as New Testament believers, we don't have to wait for something to happen to have joy. We can have joy when we realize that God's grace has been extended to us. When we come to realize that it is by His grace that we are saved and it is a gift freely given, then true joy takes up residence (Ephesians 2:8). We can rejoice in our hope of heaven, we can rejoice that Jesus will come again, and we can rejoice that the kingdom of darkness is eternally defeated. Why? Because, like the simple song says, "for the Bible tells me so."

By faith, we can look at any circumstance, see what God has promised about it, and rejoice! If we know God's will and are walking in His purposes, then we have a great deal of room for His joy, regardless of how things appear. For faith is the substance of things hoped for, the evidence of things not seen (Hebrews 11:1).

It was an extremely hot July in Canada where I was preaching at a summer meeting. My birthday, June 30, happened to fall during the event. Taking a morning off, my friend Bill Fletcher and I went fishing. We found a boat on a lake with a guide named Harry who took us out. To use a biblical phrase for it, "We fished and caught nothing."

Bill had been asleep for almost an hour when I finally stretched out on the deck of the boat. I lay there, praying and complaining over the time and money wasted. To make matters worse, I had to listen to Harry who, it seemed, was cursing the name of my Lord and Savior every five minutes. While I complained, Jesus softly whispered, "I sent you here because I am going to catch a fish."

I turned my head, looked at Harry and realized what Jesus was saying. I asked the Lord to forgive my whining, sat up, and began to share the gospel with Harry. As I did, Bill woke up and prayed softly. Little did I know what was about to take place.

"Harry," I said, "you see that pole there with the line in the water? There's a hook with bait on it. Now, if a big fish took that hook and the line started playing out and you started screaming, 'set the hook,' and I did nothing, then I would never have the joy of catching that fish. Harry, you are the big fish that Jesus wants to catch today."

As I said that, the line went screeching off the reel. Harry's face turned white. "I can't believe it," he muttered, "This has to be God." Then he screamed, "Set the hook! Set the hook!"

What a joy it was for me to land an enormous trout on my birthday. Harry was astonished. He shouted repeatedly, "I can't believe it. It's the biggest rainbow trout I have ever seen in my life. It must be over fourteen pounds!"

Then, much more important than any fish, he said, "Pray for me. I want to receive Jesus."

I prayed for Harry and noticed precious tears filling his eyes as he experienced the living Christ. As we arrived back at the dock, his fishing buddies, whose boats had already come in, asked, "Harry, did you catch anything?"

"Oh," he said, "two huge fish were caught today. That preacher caught the biggest rainbow trout I've ever seen and Jesus caught me."

10

A FRESH ANOINTING

DO YOU REMEMBER the children's story of "The Emperor's New Clothes"? How a con man came to a small kingdom with a vain ruler, posed as a tailor, and made the king a new suit of clothing out of "fabric so fine that only the most refined can see it"? Because all those in the palace wanted to get ahead in the royal administration, they didn't have the courage to say that they couldn't see the fabric or the suit of clothing. They couldn't admit that they weren't refined. It would be the end of their careers. They would no longer be accepted and respected by their peers.

So the con-man tailor spun a suit out of nothing and pretended to sew these pieces together to make the king's garment. Then, on the great day of presentation, the king decided he would see who in his kingdom was refined and who was not. He called for a parade. He put on his "new suit" and walked completely naked into the village.

For more than three quarters of the route, no one said a word other than "oohs" and "ahs" of admiration. They were all too ashamed to admit that the emperor was without clothing. What would everyone else have thought? This went on, of course, until a small boy who knew nothing of what was refined or why he should lie, pointed his finger and shouted, "The emperor has no clothes!" At this point the entire crowd saw through the ruse and began to laugh uproariously. The emperor responded by grabbing a coat from someone to cover himself, and stole back to the palace in shame. The truth had set them all free!

Paul warned Timothy there would be a time in the church when people would not listen to the true teaching but would find many more teachers who please them by saying the things they wanted to hear (2 Timothy 4:3-4). Like the emperor in the story, some ministers often parade new messages before a congregation—claiming a special anointing or a unique touch of God upon their lives—hoping for big offerings or greater acclaim. They teach messages that comfort the fleshly desires of people or make promises of what God will do if they only give offerings large enough to really show their faith in God.

Pastors parade new programs, ushering in seeker-sensitive messages that neither offend nor convict. Such things as respect, compassion, and physical well-being should not be ignored. However, a person who does not know Christ should never be made to feel at home in the church. It is the convicting power of the Holy Spirit that draws a person to Christ, not the music or the message.

Whole denominations have proclaimed the standards of the Bible outdated and have welcomed perversion into their midst. It is time someone stood up and said, "The preacher has no anointing!" Millions of Christians in America today have accepted outer religious appearances in place of the real Spirit of God. Although believers claim to have received more revelations of God today than in any previous generation, we can't seem to move past self into the supernatural power available to us. If we are more enamored with outward appearances rather than Jesus dwelling within us, then we are white tombs—beautiful and clean on the outside, but filled with deadness within (Matthew 23:27). Paul wrote:

> But realize this, that in the last days difficult times will come. For men will be lovers of self, lovers of money, boastful, arrogant, revilers, disobedient to parents, ungrateful, unholy, unloving, irreconcilable, malicious gossips, without self-control, brutal, haters of good, treacherous, reckless, conceited, lovers of pleasure rather than lovers of God, holding to a form of godliness, although they have denied its power; Avoid such men as these (2 Timothy 3:1-5, NASB).

Far too many Christians today are more interested in using Christianity to get what they want out of life rather than allowing Christ to use them to reach a lost and dying world. We want a religion that justifies us and makes us feel better about ourselves, rather than religion that transforms us into the image of Christ.

PLAIN AND SIMPLE TRUTH

We—the entire body of Christ—have become too easily lulled into fleshly complacency and spiritual poverty. We are caught up in our accomplishments rather than Christ's ministry. We no longer love truth; only what the truth can do for us. When truth is inconvenient, we ignore it. Or, as has become the norm today in business, politics, and the church, we spin the facts the way we want them.

Sometimes there is not much difference between putting things in their best light and lying. Those who spin the facts are more interested in appearance than substance. Another level of truth is what is actual and factual, plain and simple. We know how difficult being truly objective is in a situation, but those who have been with Jesus should be the most objective people on earth. They should be able to be completely honest with themselves, knowing their own faults and shortcomings, and speaking to their own hurt if necessary, for the sake of the truth.

Perhaps education has been a good example of this. In the past, teachers have been instructed to be very critical of students as if the harder they were on them, the better. Yet we found this to be damaging to the self-confidence of students. It follows suit that poor self-confidence leads to poor marks. More recently, teachers are trained to be very positive, no matter what the students does, to build their confidence, hoping that eventually this will lead to overall improvement. What in fact has happened is that we have a generation of students who now confidently make mistakes, and when confronted often scoff at the rebuke.

This positive spin is seen repeatedly in the business world. Large corporations, so intent on presenting a positive outlook to shareholders, have gone from putting things in the best light to misreporting the numbers and lying about the value of their companies. We have seen the same thing in the church. Ministers refuse to admit their human frailties until a point of total meltdown has been reached. They are then forced to step down from the pulpit because of sin or burnout.

The Bible, however, doesn't tell us that being constantly critical or always looking at things in a positive light is the answer to growing up in Christ. Ephesians instead advises us:

> That we henceforth be no more children, tossed to and
> fro, and carried about with every wind of doctrine, by
> the sleight of men, and cunning craftiness, whereby they
> lie in wait to deceive; But speaking the truth in love, may
> grow up into him in all things, which is the head, even
> Christ (Ephesians 4:14-15, KJV).

It is the truth that will set us free in every situation, and not the truth as seen through rose-colored glasses, which often distorts the facts. I believe this is one of the reasons Jesus told us to judge not (Matthew 7:1). When we add to the truth, we put ourselves in a position to be judged just as executives from big business are judged in our courts for accounting misrepresentations. We need to get back to the basic wisdom of Joe Friday on "Dragnet" so many years ago, "Just the facts, ma'am."

Let your statement be, "Yes, yes" or "No, no"; anything beyond these is of evil (Matthew 5:37 NASB).

Let your yea be yea; and your nay, nay; lest ye fall into condemnation (James 5:12, KJV).

IT IS TIME TO REPROGRAM

Of the thousands of decisions we make daily, how many do we consciously consider before acting upon them? Chances are, very few. What is directing our lives then? Habit; patterns accepted over time are repeated and justified. They become so ingrained that we don't even think before we act. We are trained by what we accept as true, and that training becomes an instinctive reaction that directs our every step. Then if those things that we have accepted are half-truths, we stumble around in the dark rather than scrutinizing them through the light of God's Word!

Such deception rarely goes from point A to point Z in a moment. Seldom does a person start in the ministry one day and the next is in bed with someone else's spouse! Rarely does a hard-working employee begin a new job with the long-range goal of embezzling from the company. Who would even consider marrying someone who they knew would someday commit murder? Though we could never imagine such things in the beginning, these things happen daily in our society—and in the church! Pastors run off with their secretaries; ushers pocket money from the collection plates; loving spouses abuse their mates for one reason or another. "If then the light within you is darkness, how great is that darkness!" (Matthew 6:23).

The acceptance of a half-truth is like smoking a cigarette. Little by little as we inhale, the nicotine darkens our lungs. After years and years of this, they turn black and can't be penetrated even by x-rays. Smoking weakens our breath and ages us prematurely. Illness creeps in until we are no longer of use to our families and those who depend on us. Sin, like cancer, grows until it takes over our entire life. Acceptance of these lies sears our conscience to the point that the voice of God no longer can penetrate the heart—the black lump within.

However, sin is not the only problem. Just as cancer is the result of taking in smoke from cigarettes, sin is the result of ingesting the half-truths that justify self on the throne. It is flesh carried away by lusts that brings about sin (James 1:15). Sin is the fruit, flesh is the root. When we repent of sin, we're dealing with the fruit, which is very important. But cutting out the root, which is self on the throne, is even more important.

Most Christian leaders, myself included, have preached against the fruit of the flesh—lying, lust, and greed. Great numbers of people go to the altar, pull the fruit off their flesh, and two weeks later return to the same altar having committed the same sins. Repentance must deal with the root. If we deal only with pruning the branches, allowing the tree to live, we only guarantee a bumper crop of sinful fruit for the next revival!

John the Baptist said one was coming to lay the ax to the root of the tree (Matthew 3:10). We don't just want to prune a little cruelty or lying. No matter what we do to the fruit of sin, if the ax is never laid to the root, we miss the reason Jesus came. We must sever the flesh root and become grafted into the true vine of Christ. Truth is the ax which will separate the root from the rotten fruit.

It is the Holy Spirit who gives us the power to see our flesh from an eternal standpoint. Flesh-fed Christians have boasted, "There is therefore no condemnation to them which are in Christ Jesus," but never realize that the rest of that Scripture is, "who walk not after the flesh but after the Spirit" (Romans 8:1). We must become absorbed in the truth of God's Word—renewing our minds. As Paul wrote in Romans 12:2:

> And do not be conformed to this world, but be transformed by the renewing of your mind, that you may prove what *is* that good and acceptable and perfect will of God.

Habit can be reprogrammed to work in our favor.

You have been believers so long now that you ought to be teaching others. Instead, you need someone to teach you again the basic things about God's word. You are like babies who need milk and cannot eat solid food. For someone who lives on milk is still an infant and doesn't know how to do what is right. Solid food is for those who are mature, who through training have the skill to recognize the difference between right and wrong (Hebrew 5:12-14 NLT).

In other words, if we feed on God's Word and grow up in Him, there will come a time that even our physical senses will know the difference between good and evil and act accordingly without a second thought. That is flesh dominated by the Spirit. This is truly life with Jesus completely on the throne of our lives. It is time that we grow up enough to accept the meat of the Word and make a lasting difference for His kingdom on the earth.

DO YOU LOVE TRUTH?

In speaking of the end times and those who would follow false prophets, the Bible tells us:

They perish because they refused to love the truth and so be saved (2 Thessalonians 2:10).

If we say we have fellowship with Him and yet walk in darkness, we lie and do not practice the truth (1 John 1:6, NASB).

Do we truly love truth? Those who risk being one with Jesus will find that His light will reveal much in their life that is harmful and should be abandoned; yet the good fruit that comes from His Spirit will thrive in this light. Jesus on the throne will shine this light into every corner and expose everything that needs to be changed or eradicated. This is exactly what needs to happen if we are to be sanctified and set apart for His use.

This is not something that will happen overnight, neither will we arrive at a place where one day we can sit down and say, "Now I am holy." It is an everyday pruning process we must go through and that always hurts. But the opportunities to have Jesus truly work through us to touch other lives makes it all worthwhile. I can imagine nothing greater than meeting Jesus on that day when I too have finished my race (2 Timothy 4:7-8) and hear Him say, "Well done, thou good and faithful servant: thou hast been faithful over a few things, I will make thee ruler over many things: enter thou into the joy of thy lord," (Matthew 25:21, KJV). It is time to draw close to God, allowing His truth to set us free from anything that might keep us from accomplishing His plan for our life on earth.

SAVOR THE GLORY

On the Day of Pentecost, people from many nations were saved and the foundation of the church was established in the known world through the testimony of those in Jerusalem. In less than 300 years, the Roman Empire, which had ruthlessly persecuted Christians for much of its history, was thought of as a Christian empire. In the first centuries, God touched various men who sought Him—Polycarp in the church at Smyrna, an African named Tertullian, an Egyptian named Antony, and others. God's power was also seen dramatically, if only occasionally, in the fourth and fifth centuries as an Italian, Jerome, translated the Bible into Latin, and the Libyan Augustine, wrote the classic, *Confessions.*

Throughout the Dark Ages, Christian slaves who were shipped to other parts of the world spread the Word of God and revival came to their captors. A young slave named Patrick escaped, but then returned to his former masters in Ireland with the power of God upon his life. The nation was transformed by the gospel of Jesus Christ. In the fourteenth and fifteenth centuries, God's power again became more evident. In England, the outpouring of the Holy Spirit influenced a young man, John Wycliffe, to translate the Bible from Latin to English. A hundred years later, William Tyndale introduced a new English Translation from the original Greek. Around this time, a German, Martin Luther, saw the corruption in the Catholic Church and sparked an entirely different kind of revival when nailing his famous Ninety-Five Theses to a chapel door in Wittenberg.

The nation of India saw flames of revival in the sixteenth century. In one instance, a minister named Francesco ordered bystanders to open the day-old grave of a dead man. The holy man fell to his knees, prayed, and commanded the dead man to rise. The man arose in perfect health—and the whole village turned to God.

Moravian exiles saw revival in Germany in 1727 when a regular meeting was disrupted and all 50 in attendance fell under the power of God. They established a 24- hour prayer chain, which remained unbroken for 100 years. Their missionaries greatly influenced two ordinary brothers named John and Charles Wesley.

In 1739, God touched the Wesley brothers and revival spread in Europe. George Whitfield, who fell under the power of God at their meetings, preached the first open-air sermon in England in 400 years. People cried out under the power of God in his services—something that troubled the 24-year-old evangelist. But a countess wrote to him, "Don't be wiser than God. Let them cry out. It will do a great deal more good than your preaching."

In the meantime, at least 50,000 people, one-fifth the entire population, were converted in New England between 1737 and 1741, as God used a young evangelist named Jonathan Edwards. This revival touched a young student at Yale College, David Brainerd, who left school to minister to the tribes of the greatly feared Native Americans. God's power that enveloped his meetings was described as "a mighty rushing wind."

The "Great American Awakening" started unexpectedly on a Sunday in 1857 at an Ontario, Canada, Methodist Church when, without any call for salvation, 21 people repented and were saved. The church had no full-time minister, but the lay pastor, recognizing God's divine power, held daily services. The move led to thousands of conversions.

That same year in New York City, Jeremiah Lanphier, an ordinary businessman led by God, organized a noon prayer meeting near Wall Street. On the first day, four businessmen joined him. That grew to 20; soon the number doubled. Then the worst financial panic in history struck. Banks closed. People lost jobs. Families went hungry. Within six months, 10,000 businessmen gathered for prayer. 20 other groups evolved. At a time when the population of America was only 26 million, an estimated one million people were converted in just two years. It literally shook the nation.

In 1904, a woman in India formed prayer groups of girls, numbering 500 strong. They saw prayer answered in July 1905, when revival broke out in many Indian cities, including Bombay (now Mumbai). Two decades later in China, the Norwegian missionary Marie Monsen's prayer groups met twice daily for seven years until revival came. At roughly the same time in Rwanda and Burundi, East Africa, several discouraged missionaries called for a week of prayer and humility before God. Within a decade, 50,000 people were converted.

THE GLORY OF GOD BRINGS REVIVAL

I deviate from the traditional meaning for revival, and define it as "a supernatural visitation within the church and also within the world" (as noted earlier). It is a supernatural new awakening. Revival happens to people whose prayers are like that of Moses:

If thy presence go not with me, carry us not up hence. For wherein shall it be known here that I and thy people have found grace in thy sight? is it not in that thou goest with us? so shall we be separated, I and thy people, from all the people that are upon the face of the earth. . . . I beseech thee, show me thy glory (Exodus 33:15-16, 18, KJV).

Moses asked for God's continual presence and God responded.

SHOW US YOUR GLORY

The Westminster Confession of Faith states that the chief purpose of man is to glorify God and enjoy Him forever. Jesus' prayer in John 17 was "that they may behold my glory, which thou hast given me" (John 17:24, KJV). God's glory follows His presence and touches lives. This is true revival. Throughout history His glory has come in bursts as individuals have yearned for God's presence. As we have just seen, amazing revivals would break out in areas as a result, but each time they fizzled out.

The destiny of nations, as well as our individual calling, is linked inexorably to God's purpose. "For whom he foreknew he also predestined to be conformed to the image of His Son" (Romans 8:29). Our destiny is to be like Jesus. Yet even the sincerest attempts to concentrate on a single set of religious goals through willpower and self-discipline leaves life untouched. We become only partially transformed, suffering moral inequality, in which one part of our nature becomes overfed, while the other is starved. This is trying to live out our Christianity in the flesh through willpower. God's hope for our future is quite different.

> And we, who with unveiled faces all reflect the Lord's glory, are being transformed into his likeness with ever-increasing glory, which comes from the Lord, who is the Spirit (2 Corinthians 3:18).

The Greek word for "glory" is *doxa* from which we get the word Doxology. As Believers, we must show the glory of the Lord as if we were mirrors reflecting His face. Our children are often a reflection of us as parents. We absorb into our innermost being those we habitually admire. We are a product of the truth we embrace.

We cannot change ourselves just as we cannot pull ourselves up by our own bootstraps. Every person's character changes and develops as it is influenced by outside forces. Often, we have failed to place ourselves in the path of such forces. Through self-dependence, struggles, efforts, and agony, we try to control circumstances, but only Christ can change us. The Word of God speaks of clay and the potter. Clay cannot mold itself; it needs the Master Potter to transform us into His design. Jesus said:

Jesus showed us that one way to open the door is to have little confidence in our own strength. We live in a generation in which we love to boast about how much power we have. Christ always works through those who recognize how much power He has.

The fishermen who became disciples were raw, unspiritual, uninspired men. But the Bible says these ordinary, unschooled men astonished everyone because they had been with Jesus (Acts 4:13). Being with Jesus changes us. Paul was immersed in Christ. When we intently dwell in the Highest, we reflect Him: "For I am confident of this very thing, that He who has begun a good work in you will perfect it unto the day of Jesus Christ" (Philippians 1:6).

When we try to repair our damaged sense of identity, or heal the wounds of our own heart, we get ahead of the first order of business and risk placing ourselves in the center of our universe. Self-interest becomes the dominant concern. Our flesh resists even the slightest demand of the Spirit. Christ will be reflected in us with all His glory when we have dealt with our stubborn commitment to self-centeredness.

The pathway to revival is clearly marked. It begins by admitting we are not yet where we need to be with God, and then builds the desire within us to conform more closely to the image to which God has called us. It is one thing to be willing to pray, but another to become a living prayer. It is one thing to make a sacrifice, another to become a living sacrifice. We too often believe we can make a small sacrifice for Jesus, thinking that is enough, rather than obeying and being a holy sacrifice by placing control of our lives on the altar of God. Romans 12:1 teaches us to be a "living and holy sacrifice."

Christians today tend to use the phrase "God is moving," and yet you won't read of the apostle Paul telling people the Holy Spirit was moving. He just moved. I'm afraid that sometimes when people emphasize the Holy Spirit moving, He is moving right out of the building, because the attention is not on Him and His work; it is on the works of the flesh. We may have so little Holy Spirit power that we spend an enormous amount of time witnessing to each other rather than allowing the Holy Spirit to bear witness of Himself.

GOD HAS BIGGER PLANS

God has a plan to take us beyond ourselves. The church in Acts changed the world. Christians preached the Word with fire and glory; there was nothing they wouldn't do for God. There were no territorial rights, no spirit of competition, no power plays, no arrogance, and no big egos.

The great teacher E.M. Bounds said, "Programs, techniques, campaigns are utterly useless unless people are under the control of the Holy Spirit. Men are God's methods. While men look for better methods, God looks for better men." You and I can be among those for whom God is looking!

WHY REVIVAL STOPS

Perhaps the greatest question for us today is not how revival is born, but what kills it? It is hard to believe that God would reach out to His people, touch them briefly, then intentionally retreat to leave them stranded. I used to think I should be horrified by my flesh, that I should control it, squelch its evil, and discipline myself unto righteousness. But Paul went far beyond that, saying he was never surprised at what his flesh was capable of, because in his flesh dwelled "no good thing" (Romans 7:18). We need this attitude. We must allow the transcendent life of Christ to transport us beyond our flesh. Without His power, we have no power. Apart from Him, we can do nothing.

When we're squeezed, what's inside comes out. Because darkness is increasing as we move toward the end of the age, more pressure will come to bear upon every believer. The flesh has to be dealt with so only the Spirit of God emerges. Earlier I mentioned Daniel 11:32, that, "The people who do know their God will be strong and do exploits." This prophecy will be fulfilled through those of us willing to pay the price.

We cannot live until we first die—to sin and to self. This is the greatest paradox in history. The Israelites were given only one use for animal flesh—to burn it (see Leviticus 6:8-13). Daily, priests robed in ceremonial attire carried the flesh outside the camp and carefully arranged the burnt offering on the altar so that no flesh escaped the flames. They constantly added more wood to the fire. Revival today is the fire of God, sent so we can die to our flesh and become alive to His Spirit.

Why hasn't the message of repentance changed the world more? It's been preached to men and women by some of the greatest orators and ministers, with sweeping revivals following. But the spirit behind each movement died because people repented for sinful deeds, the fruit of our flesh, not the root of it, and left thinking they were holy. The battle is not sin against righteousness, but flesh against Spirit.

The Word of God calls us "children of wrath" (Ephesians 2:3) when we fulfill the desires of the flesh. We wrestle against our own flesh, and never enter the real fight, which is against principalities, powers, rulers of darkness, and spiritual wickedness in high places (Ephesians 6:12). No wonder the apostle Paul said he wanted to be delivered from this "body of death."

As punishment for murder in the Roman Empire during Paul's time, the murderer would be chained to the dead body of their victim. The murderer would live with that decaying corpse until the dead body killed the living body. The apostle Paul understood that his dead and decaying flesh would kill his spirit in much the same way.

This is the difference between religion and life: "Walk in the Spirit and ye shall not fulfill the lust of the flesh" (Galatians 5:16). What kills revivals? Religion does. Religious flesh that is manipulative, competitive, angry, jealous, and covetous. Flesh creates divisions within the church—as many, if not more, than are outside the church.

Once we've truly known Christ, human religion will never again satisfy. We'll cry out, "There has to be more!" As did the priests of old, we must daily ensure every scrap of the flesh—its entire works, its lusts, and its ego—is burned. Then the fire of revival can blaze.

Religious flesh stands at the door of the Holy of Holies with hands folded, smugly believing we have been with Jesus in our quiet times, but blocking the entrance to the glory of God. English evangelist Leonard Ravenhill stated, "A man that has been with Jesus will never fear man." That most live to please others before pleasing God testifies against them, and yet we wonder why demons do not tremble and our prayers are not answered. As long as we make people our primary preoccupation, we will be disqualified from going beyond hit-and-miss revivals to the greatest awakening the world will ever see.

We can't convince a lost and dying world to embrace the good news until we deal with the bad news, that we, God's people who have been called by His name, have not humbled ourselves. We have failed to pray. We have not sought His face. We have not repented from our wicked ways. Yet God is cultivating a people who are hungry and thirsty to give up the low life of being people pleasers to attain the life of Christ.

A lost and dying world will cry out for what we have when they see that we have been with Jesus. It will not be because of what we say, but by the glory of God manifested through our private and public lives.

Being with Jesus is for those who will pursue His presence. His private presence has always come before His public power. Noted evangelist D. L. Moody said, "Let us remove all hindrances to revival that come from ourselves. Revival must begin with us." Every time the world has seen a glimpse of Jesus from one of the great revivals, people have repented. Imagine what would happen if the world could see the life of Jesus in millions of Christians whose fires burn brightly every day. Satan fears that the body of Christ will learn to become consumed by the fire of the Holy Spirit, because it will release the glory of God like the world has never seen before. May God work in your life, and mine, as we seek the Lord with all our heart, soul, mind, and strength, and share His love with every person we can until we are united with Him.

A FINAL WORD

....

Call to me and I will answer you, and will tell you great
and hidden things that you have not known.

—JEREMIAH 33:3 ESV

JEREMIAH, the Old Testament prophet, faced trying times, not only in his personal life, but in events surrounding his beloved country. As we look at him, it seems his situation was bleak. It would have been easy for his hope to completely evaporate as he pondered where he might find the help he so badly needed. Perhaps Jeremiah even wondered where God was in all the upheaval.

Then God reassured His servant that all he had to do was call upon Him, and He would answer. The Lord reminded Jeremiah that not only does He know the future; He holds it securely in the palm of His all-encompassing hand. The prophet was uplifted and cheered by God's comfort and hope during both a national and a personal predicament. Jeremiah 33:3 reminds us that God knows all, sees all, and is in control of all.

Our heavenly Father doesn't promise that troubles will not come, but He does promise that He will walk through them with us. And, after all, it is in the valley that He restores our soul.

BOOKS BY: MIKE EVANS

Israel: America's Key to Survival

Save Jerusalem

The Return

Jerusalem D.C.

Purity and Peace of Mind

Who Cries for the Hurting?

Living Fear Free

I Shall Not Want

Let My People Go

Jerusalem Betrayed

Seven Years of Shaking: A Vision

The Nuclear Bomb of Islam

Jerusalem Prophecies

Pray For Peace of Jerusalem

America's War:The Beginning of
    the End

The Jerusalem Scroll

The Prayer of David

The Unanswered Prayers of Jesus

God Wrestling

The American Prophecies

Beyond Iraq: The Next Move

The Final Move beyond Iraq

Showdown with Nuclear Iran

Jimmy Carter: The Liberal Left and
    World Chaos

Atomic Iran

Cursed

Betrayed

The Light

Corrie's Reflections & Meditations

The Revolution

The Final Generation

Seven Days

The Locket

Persia: The Final Jihad

GAMECHANGER SERIES:

GameChanger

Samson Option

The Four Horsemen

THE PROTOCOLS SERIES:

The Protocols

The Candidate

Jerusalem

The History of Christian Zionism

Countdown

Ten Boom: Betsie, Promise of God

Commanded Blessing

BORN AGAIN SERIES:

Born Again: 1948

Born Again: 1967

Presidents in Prophecy

Stand with Israel

Prayer, Power and Purpose

Turning Your Pain Into Gain

Christopher Columbus, Secret Jew

Living in the F.O.G.

Finding Favor with God

Finding Favor with Man

Unleashing God's Favor

The Jewish State: The Volunteers

See You in New York

Friends of Zion:Patterson & Wingate

The Columbus Code

The Temple

Satan, You Can't Have My Country!

Satan, You Can't Have Israel!

Lights in the Darkness

The Seven Feasts of Israel

Netanyahu (a novel)

Jew-Hatred and the Church

The Visionaries

Why Was I Born?

Son, I Love You

Jerusalem DC (David's Capital)

Israel Reborn

Prayer: A Conversation with God

Shimon Peres (a novel)

Pursuing God's Presence

Ho Feng Shan (a novel)

The Good Father

The Daniel Option (a novel)

Keep the Jews Out! (a novel)

Donald Trump and Israel

A Great Awakening Is Coming!

TO PURCHASE, CONTACT: orders@TimeWorthyBooks.com
P. O. BOX 30000, PHOENIX, AZ 85046

MICHAEL DAVID EVANS, the #1 *New York Times* bestselling author, is an award-winning journalist/Middle East analyst. Dr. Evans has appeared on hundreds of network television and radio shows including *Good Morning America, Crossfire* and *Nightline*, and *The Rush Limbaugh Show*, and on Fox Network, *CNN World News*, NBC, ABC, and CBS. His articles have been published in the *Wall Street Journal, USA Today, Washington Times, Jerusalem Post* and newspapers worldwide. More than twenty-five million copies of his books are in print, and he is the award-winning producer of nine documentaries based on his books.

Dr. Evans is considered one of the world's leading experts on Israel and the Middle East, and is one of the most sought-after speakers on that subject. He is the chairman of the board of the ten Boom Holocaust Museum in Haarlem, Holland, and is the founder of Israel's first Christian museum located in the Friends of Zion Heritage Center in Jerusalem.

Dr. Evans has authored 102 books including: *History of Christian Zionism, Showdown with Nuclear Iran, Atomic Iran, The Next Move Beyond Iraq, The Final Move Beyond Iraq,* and *Countdown*. His body of work also includes the novels *Seven Days, GameChanger, The Samson Option, The Four Horsemen, The Locket, Born Again: 1967,* and *The Columbus Code.*

✦ ✦ ✦

Michael David Evans is available to speak or for interviews.
Contact: EVENTS@drmichaeldevans.com.